Bang

to

Boom

ERIK WEISE

ISBN: 979-8-9939845-0-6

DEDICATION

To my sons —

You may be too young to understand this now, but this was for you.

I hope you learn from it, and I hope you go find hard things of your own.

To the brave first responders and veterans who do this for real, and who share their knowledge with the rest of us trying to be better.

To my wife who made space for my one-percent-better without hesitation.

ACKNOWLEDGMENTS

I didn't grow up believing I would ever write a book, let alone survive the stories that made it possible. So if you're reading this page, understand something up front: none of this happened alone. Not one mile, not one drill, not one bruise, not one breath.

To my wife —

You saw the cracks before I did. You handed me space when I needed it, pressure when I deserved it, and grace I didn't earn. You're the quiet center that made the loud parts survivable. Thank you for pushing me toward the version of myself I kept pretending I'd get to "someday." There is no chapter stronger than the one with your fingerprints on it.

To my kids —

You are the reason I trained in the first place. Every rep, every choice, every hard weekend in the desert was really a promise to you: I will come home better than I left. If this book gives you anything, I hope it's this—your dad didn't chase the heroic. He chased being responsible. And responsible wins.

To my brother, Jarrod —

This book doesn't exist without you. You were there for the first "let's do something dumb but useful," the first dusty rep at Marauders, the first door breach, the first panic, the first laugh, the first "holy shit, that worked," the first everything. Thanks for being the man beside me when the world got loud, confusing, or stupid. Thanks for dragging me forward when I stalled, clowning me when I earned it, and listening when I couldn't hide. The story is ours. The voice is mine. The courage was shared.

To the instructors who shaped my edges —

Marauders: Thank you for being the forge. For the dusty village, the smoke, the bruises, the "again," the "that'll get you killed," and the thousand little corrections that made big things possible.

Sheepdog Response: Thank you for the mat, the panic, the knives thrown into fights at the exact wrong moment, the pressure that cracked me open, and the reminder that survival is built in inches, not swagger.

Haley Strategic: Thank you for the simulator that didn't care about my feelings, the science that didn't care about my confidence, and the quiet reality that made me honest. You showed me how fear behaves, and what presence actually costs.

Fred: Thank you for the day you dropped into my truck without a word, for teaching me patterns instead of paranoia, and for showing me what real-world protection looks like when ego gets out of the way.

To the role-players, medics, LEOs, and instructors whose names I won't publish: Thank you for the trust. Thank you for letting a civilian stand close enough to feel the weight of your world. Thank you for the conversations behind vehicles, during water breaks, in parking lots, and under buzzing lights—conversations that shaped this book more than any drill did.

To Brandy: You carried a mission on shoulders that weren't built for rest. You answered midnight messages with clarity, held the Fund together with grit, and believed in us before we believed in ourselves. We're still showing up. We always will. That's how we honor you.

To everyone who has ever trained beside me: Thank you for the bruises, the laughs, the warnings, the jaw-clenching silence during night ops, and the small acts of encouragement that never make Instagram but change people anyway. When the dust settled, it wasn't the reps I remembered—it was the people.

To the readers: This was never meant to be a manual.

If anything, it was a flare shot into the dark in case someone out there needed permission to chase their own hard thing.

I hope something in these pages nudges you toward the edge of whatever scares you. I hope you try something you suck at and go too far on purpose. I hope you give yourself one moment of reckless faith — the kind that makes you feel alive again — and ride that wave until it throws you somewhere new.

If this story did anything, I hope it reminded you that courage isn't clean. It's messy, uncomfortable, and usually inconvenient. But it's worth it. Every bruise. Every breath. Every step.

Go find your hard thing. Then go all in.

FOREWORD - I WASN'T CUT OUT FOR THIS

This book doesn't start with a war story. It starts with a phone call. And not the kind you ever forget.

I was at work—real life, tucked-in shirt, Outlook calendar, the whole thing. I stepped outside to take a call from a police officer who got my number through a small nonprofit I volunteered with. His voice was steady until it wasn't. He told me about a shooting. Officer-involved. A kid. The words landed like loose gravel in my chest.

Somewhere in that conversation, two truths lined up like sights: This work mattered. And I was in way over my head.

Here's the thing: I'm not military. I'm not a cop. The closest I'd ever come to a uniform was Little League. I didn't grow up with war stories around the table or a flag folded in a shadow box on the mantle. I'm a regular guy—husband, dad, mortgage, grocery list, the kind of man who carries everyone else's leftovers to the car and forgets where he parked.

So why am I writing this? Because a strange thing happened after that call. The old seed I'd buried—the one from a nineteen-year-old's ride-along where someone handed me a badge that wasn't mine—woke up. Not loud. Just... present. I realized I could either keep pretending I was fine, or I could do something about the gap between who I was and who my family might need me to be.

I didn't wake up the next morning an operator. I didn't buy a plate carrier and become useful by Amazon Prime. I started showing up. To classes I wasn't sure I could pass, taught by people whose résumés sounded like movie trivia. I trained with law enforcement, military veterans, medics, fighters—men who could kill you with a spoon and then hand you water and mean both with love. I learned to move, to think, to breathe when everything wanted to hurry. I learned the difference between looking prepared and being useful. I failed. A lot. Some of it was hilarious; some of it stung. I once rolled with a refrigerator-sized cop in a Jiu Jitsu gym and had a full panic attack while trying not to die politely. I've been tased in a simulator because a stucco house on a screen looked too much like the one I live in. I've run toward doors I wanted no part of and through smoke that made sense only later. Every time, the lesson was the same: stress is a mirror. It shows you exactly who you are, whether you like it or not.

If you're looking for a manual, this isn't it. It won't teach you to clear a room with a toothbrush or how to win the internet with your gear flat lay. This is a map. Not a how-to, but a why-we-do. A map drawn in sweat, fear, and a few good laughs—charted by two friends who decided "someday" is a fantasy and "show up" is a plan. The truth is, I didn't start training because I thought I was tough. I started because I knew I wasn't. I wanted to be the kind of man who is useful on the worst day in the room. Useful when someone's bleeding. Useful when the doorbell rings at midnight. Useful when my kid is scared and my voice needs to be calm before my hands are clever. If there's a single promise running through these pages, it's this: I will not outsource my responsibility to the people I love.

This book follows the road we actually took. And I didn't walk it alone. The early weekends where I was the tourist who thought repetition made me dangerous. The plateau where I realized I wasn't getting better—just louder.

Then the pivot into training that cut closer to real life: executive protection in crowded places where nothing is staged and everything counts; parking-lot awareness blocks that change how you enter a grocery store; medical and movement and decision-making under pressure so the mind doesn't abandon the body when it matters.

You'll see the moments I'm proud of and the ones I'd rather hide. You'll see where ego cost me, where humility paid out, and where training bled into ordinary life in ways that had nothing to do with guns. You'll see me learn—slowly, imperfectly—that being an immediate responder has less to do with chest-thumping and everything to do with building a life that doesn't crumble when the lights flicker. If you're reading this because you think you're already the hero, I have bad news. Heroes are busy. They don't usually write books. But if you're here because something in you is restless—because you feel the distance between your best intentions and your actual capability—then you're in the right place. I wrote this for the civilian who knows he's unprepared and decides to fix it anyway. For the mom who keeps a tourniquet in the minivan and prays she never needs it. For the dad who looks at his kid across a dinner table and quietly promises, "I will be enough."

We trained. We sweated. We panicked. We got smoked and laughed and came back the next weekend anyway. We failed forward—one percent at a time—until "someday" turned into "today" and "not me" turned into "I'm here." If you're waiting for permission, stop. You don't need it. Start where you are. Start small. Start tired. Start broke. Because sooner or later, the world will test you whether you trained for it or not. Just start. Because the calendar isn't going to save you, and confidence you didn't earn won't show up when you call its name.

This book won't make you an operator. It won't make you famous. It won't even make you interesting at parties. But it might give you a language for the quiet promise you've been trying to keep. It might give you a way to measure progress that isn't Instagram. And it might convince you of the simplest, hardest truth I know: You don't have to be the best to be useful. You don't have to be fearless to be responsible. You just have to stay in the fight. I wasn't cut out for this. That's exactly why I started. And if I can do this—with a mortgage, a dad bod, and no idea what I'm doing—so can you. That day on the phone taught me the cost of not being ready. What follows is how I chose to pay it. One weekend at a time. One percent at a time. Until the man I wanted to be could finally stand in the same room as the man my family needed.

PROLOGUE - THE FIELD TRIP FROM HELL

I was nineteen the first time someone handed me a badge that wasn't mine.

No briefing. No waiver. No "welcome to government property" orientation video. Just a plain-clothes cop unhooking his metal authority, pressing it into my palm, and saying, "Clip this on your belt. Act as if. Don't talk to anybody."

Copy that.

I slid the badge on like it might bite. The room smelled like old coffee and floor cleaner—the fluorescent hum a kind of low-grade interrogation. Doors buzzed. Printers chattered. People pretended not to see each other. I followed my guy because that felt safer than standing still. He parked a cuffed man in a chair and we went to war with a stack of forms. I wrote like a liar who didn't want to get caught, trying to make my handwriting look like it paid taxes.

I wasn't supposed to be there. I knew it. He knew it. The badge knew it.

"Probably not," he said when I whispered it out loud, like we were sharing a joke that could get us both fired from jobs I didn't even have.

We finished. The system accepted us. Doors buzzed again. On the way out, he held out his hand without looking and I unclipped the lie. The steel felt warm, like it had learned my name and promised not to use it.

Outside, he laughed that tired cop laugh people learn when adrenaline and paperwork share a bed. "Thanks. Also... keys. Reunite me." He patted every pocket like a man who loses things for a living and somehow always finds more trouble instead.

It was still daylight, but it felt like midnight.

And this wasn't even how the day started.

THE MORNING BRIEF YOU DON'T IGNORE

Rewind. I showed up for a ride-along like every other civilian who thinks curiosity plus courage equals a good story. I expected seatbelt time and maybe a traffic stop. He handed me a radio. "You shouldn't need it. If you do, ask for help." The kind of sentence that makes your stomach try to climb out your throat.

Then he put me in an unmarked car. Street clothes. No decals. The vibe was, "we're not supposed to be seen but we'll be everywhere." That's when the tickle in my brain turned into a drum. This wasn't "observe and report." This was "keep up and don't die of surprise."

We rolled out with multiple units—marked cars and more unmarked, a small parade that pretended to be nothing. Destination: a known drug house in a crowded downtown area. The plan: a no-knock search warrant. The part where half the internet becomes a lawyer. I had a radio and zero business. Nineteen years old and the most dangerous thing I'd done that week was argue about lacrosse sticks at a sporting goods store.

We staged behind a sun-burned wall that crumbled if you looked at it hard enough. The marked units stacked at the door like they'd rehearsed it a thousand times—which they had. My guy and the other plain-clothes posted behind cover. I tried to be smaller than my shadow.

The knock came in the form of everything happening at once. It went smooth—blessedly. No return fire, no screaming, no flash of a weapon that makes you reconsider oxygen. The suspect got pulled out, cuffed, and I learned the first real rule: ambience lies. On the outside, it looked like order. On the inside, everyone was doing calculus on bad options and hoping the answer wasn't you die now.

THE HOUSE

"Help us look," one of the plain-clothes said, like we were at a friend's apartment trying to find a lost remote. They handed me a category—what to look for, what not to touch—and pointed at a room like they were assigning chores to the dumbest roommate.

I looked because they told me to. Behind the TV: a stash of ammo. "Hey, guys—ammo!" Like a Labrador that found a shoe and expects a medal. It was absurd. It was also useful. Those two can live together, apparently.

Out front, a uniform parked the homeowner—a drug-house landlord by job description if not HR title—on the curb in cuffs. "Watch him," the officer told me, and then he went back inside. Just me and a man in bracelets in the open air, like we'd chosen this together. Nineteen. Radio on my vest. Zero instructions beyond don't let him go anywhere. I stood there, trying to look official, trying not to look at the neighbors who were trying not to stare.

The street had that late-morning heat that makes everything smell like hot plastic. If you'd paused the day right there and asked me what I wanted to be when I grew up, I would have said alive.

They loaded the suspect. Someone shouted something. The momentum of the day pushed me into the next scene whether I liked it or not.

THE BADGE AGAIN (WITH FEELING)

Fast cut back to the booking room. Same fluorescent. Same buzz. Same illegal-by-vibes energy. The badge pressing a dent

into my skin. "Act as if," he said. So I did. We signed things.
We pretended harder than most people ever have to.

"Probably not supposed to be here," I said again, because if
you say a thing twice it sometimes becomes a prayer.

"Probably not," he said. And the printer said whirrr and
didn't care either way.

When we stepped back outside, the city had moved four
inches to the left. Lunch was next, because even chaos has to
eat. A crowd of uniforms and not-uniforms swallowed
burgers like medicine. Law enforcement quantum
mechanics: the same faces were inside, outside, and already
at the next call.

THE DARK STREET

"You still want to see patrol?" he asked. He said it like this
matters. The word landed heavy.

We tread into darker streets. "This is part of it," he said,
parking where the streetlights forgot to show up. "You run
plates." That was the job in that moment: drift, look, ask the
system questions.

An unassuming car slide past, and he read the plate out loud.
I typed. The return banged into the windshield: doesn't
match.

He nodded like gravity had been confirmed. "That's not the
right plate," he said, and that's when everything stopped
being a ride-along again and became something with teeth.

We lit him up. Sirens did their red-blue dance on a wall that
had seen decades of bad decisions. The driver did that slow,
hopeful roll that says if I move like syrup, legally it's not
happening. We stepped out. My feet sounded wrong on the

pavement. He did the talk. "Plates don't match. Anything in the car I should know about?"

The driver's mouth said no the way people do when the truth is 'please don't look at the truth.' Then he said the words that should come with a warning label: "Well... hang on."

There's always a hang on.

We looked. We found what hang on usually means. Suspended license. Wrong plates. Drugs. A car that wasn't going home. A driver who wasn't either. It wasn't TV. It was paperwork with handcuffs. But the shape of it was the same, and the outcome had weight.

No cheering. No high fives. Just the knot in my stomach pulling tighter, the knot with a heartbeat.

THE CUTAWAY: SUBURBIA

This is the part where a narrator would tell you I grew up hard. I didn't.

It was suburbia—Oregon for a while, then Arizona, team sports and dumb haircuts. Lacrosse found me in high school and taught me how to breathe as a unit. I had buddies who taught me trouble and parents who taught me better. No soldier uncles at Thanksgiving. No patrol stories at the dinner table. Just a regular kid who liked the idea of helping and was drawn to things that felt a little dangerous because they hummed louder than the rest of life.

That's how you end up nineteen with a radio on your chest and a face that looks like it should be working at Best Buy.

THE CURB, REPLAYED

Back to the curb. The cuffs. The instruction: watch him. The officer stepping away because something else needed him more. Me pretending I knew what to do if anything happened. The suspect talking, the way people talk to stay human in a moment designed to make them an object. Me nodding like my head was the only tool I had left.

When you're nineteen, your body learns things your brain can't name. Mine learned the sound of a quiet block where everything is unsafe and nobody doing anything wrong can fix it. It learned that a radio is both a solution and a dare. It learned how heavy don't screw this up feels in your bones.

THE LONG DAY

The hours blurred, the way hours do when the city keeps confessing. Another stop or not—my memory stacks them like old newspapers. What I remember is the feel: the windshield turning back into glass after being a story for too long; the radio turning down and all the adrenaline asking for an exit; my guy glancing at me like a coach deciding if the rookie has a future.

"What'd you think?" he asked. He meant the whole thing. The door. The booking. The stop. The parts where I did too much. The part where I didn't do anything and that was the job.

"It was crazy," I said. "Crazy fun. Crazy cool."

Then the truth crawled out of my mouth before my pride could catch it: "Maybe it's not for me."

He nodded like that was a right answer you don't get often. "Yeah," he said. "Happens."

We drove in a silence that wasn't empty. The radio filled it with other people's emergencies.

THE SHOWER

At home, the adrenaline took its slow apology. I showered too long, like hot water could edit memory. Over the next week I told the story to friends and we laughed where you're supposed to laugh. The punch line was always the badge warming against my hip and me not talking to anybody. "Act as if," I'd say, and everyone would do the no way face because I look like a guy who updates your router, not a guy who gets told to pretend to be the state.

It became a barbecue story. That's how civilians process miracles and felonies—turn them into comedy and pass the tongs.

THE DETOUR

Then I did the thing that doesn't make for good TV: I walked away.

No slammed doors. No "you can't handle me" speeches. I just chose a desk, a calendar, and technology sales. For a while I built home theaters for rich people and learned that wiring is therapy if you do it slow. I met a couple of pro athletes who said thanks and a couple who didn't. I stacked paychecks and unstacked sleep. The public part of my life looked like competence.

But that day planted a seed.

It idled under everything. Not loud. Not dramatic. Just a small engine in another room. Sometimes I'd catch myself standing with my back to a wall in a restaurant and call it habit. Sometimes sirens on TV would make my chest feel busy and I'd change the channel because dinner shouldn't have a heart rate.

FIVE YEARS LATER (A FLASH OF THE FUTURE)

Five years later I would walk into a gun show and say, "Let's do something dumb but useful," and find men who could kill you with a spoon and then hand you water and mean both with love.

Five years later I'd step off a rope with a rifle on my chest because a stranger told me to trust the gear.

Five years later I'd take UTMs in the ribs and learn how much the word non does in non-lethal.

Five years later I'd stand in a Walmart parking lot at midnight with instructors who hunt patterns for a living and feel my brain rearrange itself into something more useful.

Five years later I'd stand in a simulator, see a stucco house that looked like the one I live in, freeze, miss, and take a cut-rate tase to the soul because stress is a mirror and I didn't like what it showed me.

But none of that would make sense without this.

Without nineteen. Without the wall, the door, the curb, the plate that didn't match, the badge I gave back. Without learning that ambition without honesty is cosplay and I'm not built for costumes.

THE TRUTH OF IT

Most origin stories punch a hole in a wall. Mine filled out forms.

Most beginnings are loud. Mine was fluorescent.

If this book has an entrance, it's a door that buzzed open on a room where I didn't belong and asked me if I could sit very still and be useful without becoming a liar to myself.

I passed the first test by walking away.

And then, years later, I came back the right way. Not to be a cop. Not to cosplay. To train. To show up. To become responsible in a way that sticks when nobody's watching.

Not with a badge.

With intention.

With a friend.

With a plan to be better at being responsible for the people I love.

"Act as if," he told me.

I did. Then I learned to act like myself.

And that's when the real story start

THE STUPID IDEA THAT CHANGED EVERYTHING

Have you ever walked into a place that smells like freedom, diesel, and regret all at once?

Welcome to the gun show.

County fairgrounds. Late morning. Asphalt melting under boots.

Every square foot crammed with tables stacked higher than sin—Hello Kitty tasers beside German Mausers, bulk ammo by the pallet, beer-can-shaped knives, prepper gadgets that look like they were welded together in a bunker.

It's a state fair that mated with The Walking Dead and got custody of every tactical T-shirt in America.

The air smells like canvas soaked in diesel, left in the sun, sprinkled with cigarette ash and a pinch of nacho cheese.

That's how you know it's authentic.

You wade through the crowd—guys in plate carriers buying jerky, moms pushing strollers past flamethrower booths, someone trying to sell a suppressor next to a bacon-festival sign—and you realize something:

Everyone's here to *buy* equipment.

Nobody's here to *learn*.

Table after table of stuff that promises safety without sweat.

Holsters, slings, trauma kits still in plastic.

But not one booth teaching people what to actually do with it.

Then, by total accident, we see a banner tucked in the back corner:

MARAUDERS TACTICAL — CIVILIANS WELCOME.

Between a booth selling pewter dragons and one hawking beef jerky shaped like AR-15 magazines.

We stop.

Read the flyer.

"SpecOps Challenge. Learn room-clearing, explosives, repelling. Train like you mean it."

It sounds ridiculous.

So of course we sign up.

That's how it started.

No manifesto. No master plan.

Just two regular guys who'd seen one too many YouTube videos and thought, *let's do something dumb but useful*.

THE BIRTHDAY IDEA

My birthday was coming up, and I didn't want dinner or socks.

I wanted a story.

I told Jarrod, "Let's go get trained by the kind of guys who won't let us quit halfway through."

We roped in two friends. Four of us. One weekend.

A private class in the middle of the desert with a group we'd only found because fate—or bad Wi-Fi—pushed us to that one booth at that one gun show.

THE DRIVE OUT

The morning we left, the GPS was already giving up.

We had a janky PDF map printed from their website, the kind that looks like it was drawn during field ops by someone low on ink and hope.

"Turn left where the pavement ends," it said.

Super helpful.

An hour outside the city the asphalt just... stopped.

Dirt roads turned into ruts.

Ruts turned to washes.

Sometimes the map said go straight; sometimes it said "if it rained, good luck."

We argued about whether we were lost, but nobody turned around.

The closer we got, the quieter the car got.

Cell signal dropped.

Sky felt lower.

3

Wind picked up.

Then a hand-painted sign appeared on a half-fallen post: *TRAINING*.

All caps. No logo. No directions. Just that.

We pulled through a cattle gate into nothing—trailers, shipping containers, porta-johns, and dust as far as you could see.

Not sand—**moon dust.**

Powder-fine, gray-beige silt that floats when you walk, coats your teeth, fills your nostrils, and sticks to sweat like chalk.

Your boots turn battlefield-tan before the first hour's up.

When it's wet, it turns into cake batter and tries to eat your shoes.

Marauders wasn't just a place.

It was its own filter.

If you didn't want it bad enough, the desert made that decision for you before you ever touched a rifle.

We killed the engine.

Stepped out.

Dust swirled around our boots.

That was the moment I knew—we'd crossed into something different.

Stories had happened here.

And by the end of the weekend, we'd have one too.

4

Back Home Debrief

This didn't start because I thought I was tough.

It started because I knew I wasn't.

The gun show was the mirror.

The drive was the threshold.

And that first weekend?

That was baptism by moon dust.

I wasn't chasing adrenaline.

I was chasing ability.

Because if I'm going to carry the weight of being responsible
for other people, I better start training like I mean it.

DESERT BAPTISM

I didn't want a cake for my birthday. I wanted to do something that made my palms sweat.

So I texted Jarrod: "Let's do something dumb but useful." He replied with a thumbs up and a link to a place that looked like a forward operating base built out of shipping containers and willpower. Two weeks later, we were bouncing down a dirt road with dust kicking up behind us like a comet tail.

Marauders didn't look real from the highway. It slowly resolved from heat shimmer: stacked steel boxes, cut doors, frames that used to be ladders, a tower stitched together from old scaffolding and fresh faith. Out beyond it, the desert went on forever—flat, indifferent, and loud with wind.

Our crew for the birthday weekend was exactly the kind of team that gets a group text titled: "This will be fine." Me, My brother Jarrod, our dad, Tom—grandfather, gentle hammer, and two friends, Ben and Dan, who both had the courage to say yes and the good sense to bring extra water. None of us had military backgrounds. None of us had cop stories. We were suburban, overworked, and just crazy enough to think we should learn how to do hard things the right way.

The first thing Marauders gave us was a waiver with too many places to initial. The second was a safety brief that did not include jokes. The instructors carried that very specific quiet you only see in people who have been out where the map fades. Polite, clear, eyes that measured whether you were listening. They moved like tools being put back exactly where they belong.

We stepped into the wind and the heat stepped back onto us. The air smelled like sunblock, hot steel, and gun oil. A generator coughed alive somewhere behind the shoot house. Gravel chewed under boots. Someone yelled, "Muzzles down," and twenty strangers turned as one. I adjusted a plate carrier that didn't fit and tried not to look like the guy who was thinking about snacks this early in the day.

It wasn't a range-day field trip. It was an initiation.

ARRIVAL & INITIATION

They built us from zero. Fingers straight. Muzzles down.
Move here. Stop there. We learned to see our own
carelessness, which is a painful kind of education. Every
correction landed with the same message: go slower, be
cleaner, live longer.

Range etiquette turned into a kind of choreography. Muzzle
awareness is a posture, not a rule. You hold it with your
whole body, not just your hands. When someone said
"index," twenty rifles tilted the same safe way and the world
relaxed a little. When someone said "safe," we all pressed on
the same piece of plastic and metal and turned down the
volume on risk. Those little mechanics—finger discipline,
flagging, chamber checks—felt boring until you imagined the
alternative, and then they felt like love.

The tower looked like a dare that got popular. From the
ground, the third story felt ambitious. From up top, it felt
personal. The wind up there didn't blow—it pulled. It slipped
through the steel grating and sang in the ladder rails. You
could see forever. You could also see the ground in a way that
made your stomach talk to your brain.

"Trust the gear," an instructor said. He didn't say it like
comfort. He said it like math. I clipped in. The harness bit
into my hips. My rifle hung off a sling that suddenly felt like a
leash. Knees had opinions. Palms sweated inside gloves I had
bought because some review said they were "breathable."
Everything on me was loud. Breath. Heartbeat. Velcro that
never seemed as sticky as the day I bought it.

There is no elegant way to step off a third-story ledge in full
kit. There is only step and then gravity. Boots met
wall—knock, knock—and I walked straight down steel and
plywood while the tower shook its dust into the wind. The
rope burned a line of heat across my glove as it slid. The

desert smelled like baked dirt and old tires. When the rope came tight and popped free, my feet hit ground, and my brain reentered my body. I looked up, Jarrod looked down. He didn't shout anything inspirational. He just nodded like two brothers do when they're pretending they planned this.

We cycled through that tower until the fear got boring. By late afternoon, the sun had cooked us down to our essential ingredients. Our dad smiled the same way he does when a chore finally gets done correctly. Ben kept cracking jokes that only landed after three seconds because everyone's brains were buffering. Dan had that focused quiet of a guy stacking mental note cards.

Breaching came with humility. Movies lie. Doors are not insults you settle with a single kick. The instructors handed us the ram—the "key"—and placed us along a wall: stack, six to eight deep, roles like vertebrae. Breacher. Breacher security. Assaulters one through however many the hallway would tolerate. We were told not to be impressive, just to be correct.

My first swing was confident in the way ignorance is confident: all muscle, bad angle, poor stance. Thump. The door politely disagreed. Second swing: thump. Door remained in its career. Third swing—a small crack of surrender appeared like a coupon I didn't know I had. That six inches felt like a parade. Nobody clapped. Nobody needed to. The stack breathed together and folded around the opening like a living hinge. The ram isn't rage. It's timing at velocity. If your stance lies to you, the tool tells the truth with interest.

MICRO-DEBRIEF: BIRTHDAY WEEKEND

That night, the wind crawled through the cracks of my hotel room like it was looking for something it lost earlier. I lay there with dust still in my hair and a bruise flowering on the heel of my hand where the sling had chewed skin. My body argued for comfort; my brain kept replaying clean sequences, then dirty ones, then clean again. I fell asleep on the second or third loop and woke up with grit in the corners of my eyes and the quiet certainty that we were coming back.

THE RETURN

We came back.

Not with the same five-man birthday crew—life pulled Tom, Ben, and Dan back toward normal weekends—but Jarrod and I couldn't unknow what we'd found. So we returned to the desert on Saturdays that felt like a quiet rebellion against comfort. New students rotated in. The instructors were the same—same voices, same patience, same uncompromising safety. The village looked different every time: doors moved, walls re-cut, rooms rearranged just enough to make familiarity useless.

Follow-up weekends are where respect gets built. You stop performing bravery and start practicing competence. The desert teaches in small changes. A sling adjustment that keeps your rifle from strangling you on a sprint. A plate carrier strap you finally position where it won't chew your collarbone. A knee placement that buys your shot a second breath to be steady. None of those things win Instagram. All of those things keep the day safer for everyone near you.

We started each morning with the quiet joke of grown men rolling their shoulders like baseball pitchers, pretending nothing hurt yet. Hydration tasted like warm tin. Sunscreen stung eyes. The smell of CLP got on everything, including the sandwich you swore you wrapped properly. And still—every time they said, "Stack it up," the world reduced to roles, angles, and a promise.

THIRD STORY — THE WIND AND THE WELD

The third story looked reasonable from the ground. From up top it moved like a thing that could change its mind. The tower creaked the way old houses talk when they're lonely. Wind hissed through the grating and grabbed your kit like a thief. Fifteen, maybe twenty extra pounds pulled at places you didn't know had leverage. Your harness reminded you that gravity had lawyers.

I stared at the weld where the line was anchored and thought, I really hope the desert handyman who did this had coffee first. I don't know anything about welding. So: faith plus carabiner. "Run the line," they said. "Don't stop at the bottom. Run until it breaks free." You hear that and think it's a metaphor. Then you try to stop one step early and find out why it's a rule.

Step. Gravity. Boots on wall. Moon dust jumped up in a gray fog as my feet hit dirt. The rope popped free and I ran it out, rifle bouncing on my chest, weight pulling sideways in a way you can only fix by getting stronger. I learned I could run and breathe panic and still not die from either.

At the bottom, Jarrod laughed, the sound of two brothers daring each other to pretend that wasn't scary. "Again?" he said. We climbed.

SECOND STORY — 300 YARDS, IRON SIGHTS

We posted up in a second-story cutout that was just big enough to kneel and just mean enough to splinter a knee if you weren't careful. Earlier that day, we'd learned how to zero rifles properly. Now the instructors pointed into the desert where a silhouette waited like a dare at 300 yards.

No glass. No magnifier. Iron sights and a relationship with humility. The wind pressed at us and then let go. I settled cheek to stock, let the front sight post live where it wanted to live, breathed out the part that was ego, and pressed.

10

The sound of a 300-yard hit arrives late and thin, like gossip. The first shot was a miss. The second I don't remember. The third **ping** whispered back across the dirt and made my brain sit up. I felt like I'd punched the moon and it had politely acknowledged receipt.

Distance teaches patience. Cheek weld that doesn't float. Breathing that respects the sight picture. Press that doesn't announce itself to your whole body. Cheap white-box ammo did me no favors; I learned to care what lived in my magazines. Jarrod found his rhythm next to me, the way he always does—quietly, then decisively. We ran the lane, back to prone, adjust, press, wait, ping, smile small, reload.

We took a photo from that second-story cut-out—sweat salt tracks on our cheeks, dust painting our arms the color of the village, the kind of grin you only give a camera after the thing works and no one got hurt. I hope it makes the book. Not because we look cool. Because it's the face you make when proof meets patience.

THE STACK — "I HAVE THE ONLY KEY"

The door we trained on had opinions. The wood was tired in places and mean in others. Hinges squeaked a specific complaint. We formed a stack—six to eight deep, roles set. Breacher, breacher security, assaulters, and the guy in back who always thinks he's not doing much until he's suddenly the only one who can see the thing everyone else missed.

My turn with the ram arrived again. The tool is honest the way a mirror is honest. If your feet aren't under your hips, if your hands don't mean it, if you pick the wrong spot on the door, you lose seconds and give the room mercy it hasn't earned. "Again," the instructor said. Not angry. Absolute. Again meant do it right this time.

First swing: thump. Second: thump. Third: crack. Six inches. That was enough to make an argument. The stack sighed the way a team sighs when the plan starts to agree with reality.

11

Breacher security's muzzle owned the world that wasn't the door. Assaulter One lived at the edge of a sprint he wasn't allowed to start yet. Assaulter Two—me, often—learned to be a shadow with responsibility.

We rotated every position, not because everyone needs to master everything, but because everyone needs to understand the friction the other positions carry. Seeing the world through someone else's sight picture makes you kinder and more lethal in the right directions.

I learned the ram has recoil like a conversation you weren't ready for. If your stance lies, your shoulder will snitch on you. The fix was unglamorous: move your feet, tighten your core, hit the right spot, trust the timing. Precision looks a lot like humility in motion.

MICRO-NOTES ON GEAR (TRUE THINGS I LEARNED THE HARD WAY)

• Plate carriers don't become comfortable; they become familiar. Tighten them when you're fresh or they'll own you when you're tired.

• Gloves are a compromise. Feel versus protection. Pick your pain early so you don't discover it at the wrong time.

• Slings make you efficient or make you miserable. A two-minute adjustment saves an hour of cursing.

• Cheap magazines make expensive problems. If a spring feels like a question mark, replace it.

• Hydration that tastes like a garden hose still beats the emergency room.

• Sunscreen in your eye will make you shoot like a liar. Avoid.

THE BANG

I didn't know training flashbangs were a thing until
Marauders. I'd seen YouTube and movie sets. That's not the
same as standing in a shipping container with a metal room
echoing your heartbeat back to you while a device the size of
a soda can rewrites the air.

They laid the trainers out on a folding table like talismans.
Some were air-powered, CO_2 and small primers. Loud
enough to make a point, great for reps. The ones Marauders
loved had heavier bodies and used blanks or small blasting
caps. The difference wasn't just volume. It was presence. You
felt those in your ribs.

We weren't live-firing this block, so ear pro came off. That
sounded like a relief until the first bang taught me what a
pressure wave really is. The sequence became a kind of
music: pin pulls, spoon snaps, hard clack, half-second of the
longest silence, then 'foop'—except it isn't really a sound; it's
the room slapping the inside of your skull with its own hands.
Dust shook out of seams and made a ghost of the air for a
breath.

Speed. Surprise. Violence of action. The bang is a
punctuation mark that makes the next sentence true.

We formed the stack in a corridor of plywood and shadows.
Breacher up front with forty-five pounds of persuasion.
Breacher security making sure the world didn't enter our
world until we were ready. Assaulter One at the door, poised
to toss. I was Assaulter Two, close enough to smell the oil on
#1's sling, heart thundering loud enough to feel it in my teeth.

The ram came in like an argument. Boom. Boom. Crack. The
door surrendered an inch. Assaulter One flicked his wrist. Pin
out. Spoon snap. The world went white. Heatless light
bounced off steel and came back mean. Pressure tried to push
me through my own face. Clever thoughts disappeared. Only
training survived.

MOVE

No cinematic pause. My foot crossed the threshold and I ate the room like we were starving. #1 flowed left, so I took the opposite. Angles collapsed. Corners died. My muzzle wrote a sentence across a wall that ended with "clear." The bang creates the interval. Your job is to live inside it.

We ran that rep until the room wasn't a monster; it was geometry. Loud helped. Loud erased doubt. Loud gave the plan the only chair in your head.

PASSING THE SQUEEZE

It sounds small when you say it out loud. It feels sacred when you do it for real. In the stack, #1 pulls the pin but doesn't throw. He turns enough to find #2—just enough eye contact to say, "We're about to change the world on the other side of this door." #2—me—places a hand on his shoulder. Not a pat. A deliberate squeeze that says, "I'm with you." He squeezes back. Consent. Timing. Unity. Two people syncing to violence on purpose.

The instructors watched that moment like hawks. "Don't short it," one said. "Get it right. Then go." It wasn't ceremony. It was control. The touch sets tempo for everyone behind you. If the touch is sloppy, the entry is sloppy. If the touch is right, bodies move like a paragraph that knows where it's going.

We ran just that moment five, six times in a row: eyes, pin, squeeze, squeeze back, toss, move. The repetition scrubbed away ego. What remained was trust and timing.

Sometimes the loudest corrections arrive quietly.

NIGHT OPERATIONS — SETTING THE TABLE

Night falls fast in the desert. One moment you're squinting; the next it's ink. No city glow. No hum of power lines. Just wind and heartbeat and the occasional far-off dog deciding to be a wolf for a while.

The prep felt different. Lights checked. Lenses wiped. Batteries swapped. Someone taped a spare handheld to their chest rig because it was better to look silly than to be blind. We marked paths with chem lights because otherwise you could get lost walking to the Porta-John. Our rifle lights became lifelines—primary, secondary, backup. Safety brief went from strict to sacred. The instructors' voices took on a particular stillness. The desert answered back with a silence that made your ears invent sounds so they wouldn't feel useless.

We staged at the edge of the village. You could hear zippers and Velcro like crickets. People talk less at night. You conserve words the same way you conserve light. The cadence of the day—banter, instructions, jokes—drops into a whisper world where the only language that matters is hands and patience.

THE NIGHT SHOOT

We'd been moving since sunrise. Twelve hours? Fourteen? Time stretched and snapped back like elastic. Shoulders felt a size too small. Brain felt two sizes too big. We flipped the lights out and added live weapons, and the world shrank to the small cone in front of each of us.

The first string on steel felt like throwing darts in a closet while wearing gloves. You don't just acquire targets; you locate them. Where's the berm? Where's the steel? Where am I? Every shot sounded wrong until it didn't. And when the ping cut through the night, it felt like a signal flare: I'm still here.

Fatigue made my breathing loud inside my head. I tried to slow it. Grip tightened, then loosened—too much tension is as bad as not enough. Trigger press turned into prayer. I stopped trusting the gear and started becoming the gear. That's when it works—not when you believe the rifle will save you, but when you become too boring to make extra mistakes with it.

Then the shadows moved.

Something flickered at the edge of my vision—left of the last target stand, maybe behind it. I shifted my light, saw nothing, shifted it back, and it was there again. "Hey, did you see that?" I asked without meaning to. "See what?" Jarrod said. An instructor's voice arrived, calm enough to borrow. "You good?" "I think I'm seeing things," I said. "Perfectly normal," he said. "Stress, dehydration, long day. It happens."

He was right. I was hallucinating. My mind, overclocked and underfed, was filling the dark with whatever it thought would keep me alert—ghosts, shapes, bad guys who dissolved under light. The brain hates blank space. It paints monsters in it so you stay awake.

We kept running the line. Move. Light. Press. Reset. Move. Light. Press. The routine became a rope. Let go and the river takes you. Hold on and you arrive where you're supposed to, even if you don't remember the shoreline along the way.

Someone's handheld died. Another guy's headlamp went out and came back with a smack. Chem lights pulsed like heartbeat monitors along the path to the berm. Instructors prowled with quiet confidence, calling out safety like air-traffic control. We listened because we wanted to go home.

At some point—ten minutes or an hour later—the sky felt bigger. Temperature dropped just enough to notice. My heart rate softened between strings. I started calling small wins: good light, clean press, don't outrun the problem. When steel answered, I let the ping land and then let it go. Celebrate later. Right now, don't break the sequence that's working.

We shut down the line. Lights stayed off for a beat that felt like a held breath. Then flashlights popped on and twenty tired people turned into a small constellation. Nobody said much. When you survive your first night shoot, words feel disrespectful. We flagged rifles, cleared chambers, touched bolts out of habit, checked each other's work the way people do when they've decided to be worth the trust they're asking for.

MICRO-DEBRIEFS — TAILGATE TRUTHS

On the tailgate, I wrote notes with a Sharpie on a Rite in the Rain pad that still smells like the first time I opened it.

• Darkness will trick you into inventing stories. Don't argue with the story. Acknowledge it and do the process anyway.

• Hydrate before the desert asks you to. The question always arrives late.

• Your sling is either management or punishment. Adjust it like it decides your mood.

• Lights fail. Have backups for your backups. Practice light discipline like the beam carries your bank account.

• If you can't find the berm in your mind, don't press the trigger in your hand.

• The people next to you are not scenery. Their safety lives inside your process. Treat it like your name is on it.

Jarrod handed me water. He didn't ask if I was okay. He knows better. He looked at the village—black shapes against a darker sky—and did that quiet half-smile he does when he's choosing not to say something obvious like, "We're different now."

THE DAY AFTER

I woke up before the alarm. My hands had lines where sling and gloves had made their case against soft living. Knees hummed. Lower back sent a memo. I made coffee badly and stood by the kitchen window looking at a neighborhood that did not know how loud the night can be when you turn the lights off on purpose.

There's a shift that happens after weekends like this. You drive differently—not scared, but aware. You walk through a grocery store and notice hands before faces. You sit down at a restaurant and pick a seat that doesn't turn your back on the door without thinking you're being dramatic. You're not paranoid. You're paying attention.

I did a gear audit on the trunk. Moved a tourniquet to a pocket it should have been in already. Adjusted a strap that had been quietly murdering my collarbone for two weekends. Wrote "batteries" on a sticky note and stuck it to the inside of the lid where I'd have to see it next time we loaded up.

I don't think training makes you a different person. I think it gives the best version of you more chances to show up when the day doesn't care what you want.

MORE WEEKENDS — REPETITION AS RELIEF

We went back. Again. Same instructors. New layouts. Same rules. The tower stopped being a dare and became a tool. The second-story cutout became a classroom. The ram became heavy and honest. The flashbang became a metronome. The night became less a threat and more a filter—you learn quickly what in you is real and what you were just pretending could survive pressure.

Instructors said "Again" more than any other word. It wasn't punishment. It was mercy. "Again" is a chance to correct the thing you're now honest enough to see. "Again" is an invitation to put your ego in the truck and do the work with your hands, feet, breath, and eyes. "Again" is how ordinary people become reliable on purpose.

Between evolutions, Jarrod and I sat on tailgates and shared the kind of silence that's full of words neither of us felt like saying out loud. We talked about kids and schedules and work, and then some sentence about angles or timing would land and we'd both nod like, yes, that's the part you can't skip anymore.

VOICE NOTES TO SELF (WRITTEN LATER, KEPT FOREVER)

• Courage is controlled panic practiced until it looks like skill.

• The right amount of fear is a seatbelt. Keep it buckled.

• If you need to ask whether the muzzle is safe, it's not. Fix the posture, not just the angle.

• Speed you can't explain is luck. The desert hates luck.

• Celebrate after the truck is parked, the bolt is forward on an empty chamber, and your people are counting bruises instead of blessings.

HANDOFF

We didn't know it at the time, but everything we learned in these weekends was scaffolding for a bigger test—the one that took two days and didn't care how much sleep you thought you needed. We'd earned the right to find out what it felt like to plan an operation and live inside it until the sun forgot where it was in the sky.

That story is next.

For now, the last thing I'll say about Marauders at this stage is simple: it didn't turn us into anything we weren't. It stripped away what we didn't need and made the rest of us louder. Not with noise. With presence.

The desert didn't make me tougher. It made me quieter. And that quiet—

That's where the work lives.

BETWEEN LIGHT AND NOISE — SMALL LESSONS THAT LANDED HARD

There were a hundred little moments that don't look like much on paper but changed everything.

An instructor stopped me mid-run and rotated my hips with two fingers. "There," he said, and the next shot broke like glass instead of concrete. Another time he tapped the back of my elbow and my sight picture stopped floating like a balloon. None of it felt dramatic. All of it was expensive in the right currency: attention.

We learned to grip the rifle like a handshake you meant, not a hand you were trying to punish. We learned that breathing is a sight tool, not a habit. We learned that eyes lie when hearts panic, so make the heart bored—count cadence, call sights, press, follow through, reset, breathe. Again.

Reloads went from a hunt to a habit. Early on, I fished for magazines like my plate carrier was a junk drawer. Later, my hand went where it was supposed to go without bothering my eyes. That's the point of practice—you relocate work from your mind into your body so your mind can be a strategist and not a frantic intern.

Communication cleaned up, too. We stopped over-explaining and started naming the thing that actually mattered. "Left corner." "Window." "Door." "Up." "Moving." "Set." Brevity is kindness when heart rates are high. You learn not to make radio poetry. You learn to be useful.

Heat management was its own class. Shade becomes a resource you share. People stop hogging it. Water bottles get passed without ceremony. Somebody pours a little on the back of your neck and you pretend you're fine until you are. Hats that seemed optional at 8 a.m. turn into religion by noon. Sunscreen becomes a team sport: "You missed your ears."

Foot care decides how brave you feel. Gravel sneaks into boots like it has a key. Tape hot spots early or you'll limp heroically and learn nothing except where your pride lives. Sit in the dirt, pull a sock, clean it, laugh at yourself, and get back in the stack. There's nothing glamorous about being functional. Be functional anyway.

Safety never left the room. The instructors could feel it go soft from forty feet. One of them would step in like a shadow you didn't see coming and reset the tone. "Safe." Clicks. "Index." Angles. "Muzzle." Posture. The class became a flock that turned together. I didn't realize how much that mattered until one afternoon when everyone got tired at the same time and the staff snapped us back into attention with a voice that had gravel in it. Nobody argued. We tightened up. We earned the next rep.

You start to understand why professionals have rituals. Rituals survive fatigue when preferences fail.

THE DRIVE HOME — WHAT THE DESERT DOES TO A STEERING WHEEL

The steering wheel felt different after those days. My hands were louder—tendons talking, skin tight where sling and glove met bone. The truck smelled like dust and victory. We didn't turn on the radio. The road unspooled in long brown-gray lines and the sunset did its trick where the whole sky looks like it's burning but no one calls 911.

We talked in pieces. A correction here. A laugh there. The word "again" floating between us like a plan. We stopped for gas at a place where the floor had a story and the cashier looked like he had one too. I caught our reflections in the glass—salt crust on hats, raccoon eyes where glasses had been, that look men get when they've been reminded that work is a privilege.

Back home, the gear dump hit the living room like a small yard sale. Plates came out with noises you feel in your spine. Gloves went on the dryer like trophies. I wiped carbon from places I didn't know collected carbon and found sand in a pocket that had a zipper on it. The shower ran until the water finally negotiated with the dust on my neck. I slept facing a wall I didn't remember picking.

In the morning, the house had opinions. Kids clattered bowls. The dog forgave me for leaving. The coffee tasted like a negotiation I won. I packed the trunk better than last time because the version of me who cleans up after training deserves not to hate the version of me who loads before it.

JARROD MOMENTS — HOW BROTHERS SAY "I'M WITH YOU" WITHOUT SAYING IT

Jarrod is a study in economy. He saves energy for when it matters. He doesn't chase drama and he doesn't feed it. In the stack, that turns into a kind of gravity. He does the right thing at the right time and people orbit that choice.

There were runs where I felt the urge to rush. He'd be just behind me and I could feel his presence hold me to the plan like a hand on a shoulder saying, "Stay with it." Afterward, he'd say one sentence that cut three mistakes in half. "You stepped too deep on that first corner." "You re-gripped mid-trigger." "You didn't need that breath; you needed the next one."

He also laughs at exactly the moment laughter turns into medicine. When I hit my first 300-yard ping with irons, he didn't high-five. He nodded, smiled small, and said, "Do it again." When my first door finally cracked, he didn't shout. He moved. That's a blessing—someone who translates your wins into momentum instead of noise.

On night shoots, there's a kind of listening you can do for the people you love. You listen for their light to come on. You listen for their breathing to settle. You listen for the sound they make when steel answers them. You don't say anything about it. You just stand there, ready to hand them a battery or a bottle or a bad joke if they need it.

INSTRUCTOR LINES THAT LIVE IN MY HEAD

"Slow is smooth, smooth is fast," is a cliché until a man who has earned the right to be listened to says, "Slow is safe and safe survives."

"Again."

"Trust the gear and if you can't, fix your gear."

"You can't miss fast enough to win."

"If you don't know where your muzzle is, nobody cares what you intend."

"Don't move like you're hoping. Move like you're responsible."

"No one cares what you hit by accident."

"Hydrate like your brain is invited to this."

"Your corner isn't your identity. It's your assignment."

"Breathe."

23

Those lines built a house in my head and I keep paying the mortgage by doing what they ask.

WHY WE KEPT COMING BACK

People assume we were chasing adrenaline. We weren't. Adrenaline is loud and leaves you broke. What we wanted was ability. Ability is quiet and leaves you with receipts.

There's a dignity in being useful under pressure. It shows up in small domestic ways. When something drops and shatters in the kitchen, you don't flinch. You move your kids back with a gentle hand, you get a broom, and you handle it. When a loud noise hits a quiet room, you don't turn it into a story about danger—you turn it into a moment where you scan, confirm, and return to calm. Training bleeds into everything else in a way you can't quarantine. You become someone your future self can rely on.

And there's friendship in the repetition. The same instructors. The same jokes told by different people. The same dust finding new places to live. The same ritual of checking each other's chambers before you pack it in. Human beings aren't built to be lone wolves. We're built to be a pack that earned its own trust.

THE MOST HONEST CHECKLIST I OWN (WRITTEN AFTER WEEK FOUR)

Before leaving the house:

• Water, more than I want to carry.

• Batteries, the right ones.

• Snacks that won't melt into a punishment.

24

- Two pairs of socks.

- A willingness to be corrected without acting like it's an autobiography.

On site:

- Safety first, second, third.

- Ask smart questions.

- Do the boring things perfectly.

- Bleed in the right direction (physically if necessary, emotionally never outward).

- Laugh when it heals, not when it hides.

After:

- Clean what you used.

- Write down what you learned.

- Don't confuse fatigue with accomplishment.

- Thank the people who carried pieces you didn't see.

- Be a better dad/husband/neighbor because of this, or don't come back.

WHAT THE NIGHT TAUGHT ME ABOUT DAYLIGHT

After the night shoot, daylight felt like cheating. It took away one layer of mystery and left you with the ordinary challenge of doing simple things correctly while your heart insists on improvising. I noticed I wasted fewer words. I cut fewer corners. My walk from the truck to the firing line had a different posture to it—less "I hope this goes well," more "I'm going to do my job." I also noticed I had more patience for other people's nerves. You don't mock fear after you've met your own in a place with no lights. You learn to say, "Stand here. Breathe with me. One thing at a time." It's amazing how often that turns into progress that looks like magic and is really just kindness multiplied by practice.

THE QUIET ENDING (BEFORE THE NEXT BEGINNING)

We loaded the truck in the dark more times than I can count. Headlamps made halos out of dust. The instructors' silhouettes moved like punctuation marks in a sentence we were all writing together. Someone always left a glove on a tailgate. Someone always remembered just in time.

Leaving never felt like leaving. It felt like a handoff. From that dirt to our street. From that tower to our stairs. From that stack to our family table. The point isn't to live at the range. The point is to live better everywhere else because you learned how to be honest where the consequences are immediate.

We didn't know the full weight of what we were saying yes too. We didn't need to. We just needed the next correct thing—show up, shut up, learn, again. The bigger test had already been scheduled for men who kept their promises. It would last two days and test what stories could not. We drove toward it without seeing it yet, and the desert let us go because we had listened.

26

THE FIRST TIME THE DESERT SPOKE BACK

You ever look around and realize you're the dumbest guy in the room?

That was every Saturday at Marauders.

Week two, week three, week four—every time we showed up, we thought, "We've got this now." And every time, the universe replied: "Hold my beer."

The Marauders program wasn't just some casual "fire a few rounds and call it a day" setup. It was a system. A curriculum. A long, dusty grind that looked suspiciously like Navy SEAL Hell Week if it were run out of an abandoned paintball park in Arizona.

And we kept coming back for more.

Each weekend added another brick.

One weekend it was long guns. Next weekend—shotguns and breaching. Then UTM force-on-force. Then night movement. Then live room clears with role players who were way too good at screaming things like "Don't shoot!" while actively trying to stab you with a plastic knife.

It was like unlocking DLC packs in a Call of Duty game—except with real sweat, real bruises, and real consequences if you half-assed anything.

Repelling in full kit was where things got real.

Climbing up four shipping containers in 90-degree heat with a rifle slung across your chest and a breaching tool swinging off your back is not something I recommend unless you're getting paid or trying to impress God.

At one point, I lost my footing on the rope, spun sideways, and almost took Jarrod's head off with my rifle sling. He didn't flinch. Just looked up at me and said, "Nice of you to join us."

That's friendship.

Then came breaching.

Let me explain breaching if you've never done it. It's not like in the movies where one swift kick sends the door flying off the hinges and everyone moves like SEAL Team Six.

It's more like:

Step 1: Misjudge the hinge side.

Step 2: Get stuck in the door frame.

Step 3: Realize you forgot to rack the shotgun.

Step 4: Get yelled at by the instructor.

Step 5: Do it again. But sweatier.

Eventually, we got good at it. Good enough to hear the *crack* of a clean breach and move in with our buddies, slicing corners and calling "CLEAR" like we'd actually done something right.

Every successful door gave us confidence. Every bad run gave us humility.

UTM days were different.

Force-on-force training meant real rifles converted to shoot non-lethal marker rounds. Which is fine—until the first time you get shot in the ribs through your plate carrier and realize pain is a hell of a teacher.

The worst part? You could get shot by your own teammate if your comms were off or you cleared the wrong corner.

Ask me how I know.

The village was its own character in the story.

Built out of recycled containers, plywood, and pure madness—it was designed to disorient, confuse, and punish bad decisions.

There were alleyways that led nowhere. Buildings you could enter but not exit. Corners that looked safe until they weren't.

And it worked. Every time we thought we had it dialed, the village reminded us: "You don't."

But here's the thing: we kept coming back.

Because something about this place—this weird tactical boot camp turned DIY crucible—was giving us something we didn't know we needed.

It was showing us what it meant to learn under pressure. To fail and adapt. To push past the embarrassment and get back in the stack.

But Marauders wasn't one experience. It was a hundred micro-experiences stitched together, each one designed to expose a flaw, break a habit, or build a new one.

And no two days were ever the same.

One day you'd be clearing rooms in a three-man cell under simulated stress. The next you'd be working stairs with a full team. Then a moment later you're holding a breaching ram wondering how the hell actual SWAT guys make this look easy.

Each evolution peeled back a layer.

The more reps we got, the more we learned: you never rise to the occasion—you fall to the level of your training. And our level was rising, painfully, rep by rep.

Breaching day was when that lesson punched me in the face.

Literally.

We were running a scenario where the first man in the stack hits the door with a ram. The second man provides security. The third man calls the movement. Sounds simple, right? Wrong.

On my first run, I misjudged the angle, the ram bounced, and the recoil slammed straight into my chin.

Stars. Real ones.

Instructor looked at me and said, "Congratulations. You just knocked yourself out in a fight you started."

Humility delivered.

Every weekend had a moment like that—something embarrassing, something painful, something you'd laugh about later, but only after sitting in the car wondering if you should be trusted with adult decisions.

But the pain wasn't random. It was engineered.

If you've never been in a container maze under pressure, here's the best way I can explain it: imagine playing a video game where someone else controls the lighting, the sound, the layout, the timing, the enemy movement, and your stress level. Now imagine that when you lose, you feel it.

There were no perfect runs. Ever.

Something always went wrong.

A missed corner.

A bad callout.

A door forgotten.

A rifle snagged on a sling.

A moment of indecision that turned into a cascade of mistakes.

But gradually, very gradually, the mistakes changed. They got smaller. Less catastrophic. More recoverable.

We weren't becoming experts. We were becoming aware.

And awareness is the first real skill.

One of the instructors, a guy built like a fire hydrant who talked like a disappointed dad, pulled me aside after a sloppy run and said, "You're too polite."

Too polite.

I stood there sweating through my vest thinking, *Polite? I'm trying not to die*. But he wasn't wrong.

Politeness is hesitation wearing church clothes. In a hallway, that gets people killed.

He made me run the scenario again. And again. And again. Each time pushing faster, louder, more decisive. Less "after you, sir" and more "move."

By the end I wasn't smooth, but I was sharper. And I finally understood what he meant: decisiveness is a skill you practice, not a personality trait.

Breaching was its own form of chaos.

People think the hard part is swinging the ram. It's not. The hard part is doing it with six other people depending on you to be perfect while your brain is screaming *don't screw this up* and your hands are sweaty inside gloves that suddenly feel two sizes too small.

The instructors didn't help. They'd stand behind you, arms crossed, watching every micro-movement like human lie detectors.

"Too high."

"Too low."

"You hesitated."

"You're thinking—stop thinking."

"Again."

The ram itself felt like some ancient artifact—heavy, steel, and slightly cursed. Every time you picked it up you could feel the expectation baked into it. This wasn't just a tool; this was responsibility given shape.

The first time I landed a perfect hit, the sound was addictive. A deep *whump* followed by the door flying inward like it knew it had been defeated. The stack surged in. Corners sliced. Commands snapped. It felt like flight.

The next run, I missed the hinge, the ram bounced, and I nearly knocked myself unconscious again.

Humility is the tax you pay for competence.

UTM force-on-force brought out a different side of all of us.

There's nothing quite like the emotional roller coaster of stepping into a shoot house knowing that at any moment someone might pop around a corner and light you up with marker rounds that hit like angry hornets.

The first time I got shot, it wasn't cinematic. No heroic last stand. No slow motion. Just a sharp, humiliating *thwack* to the ribs that left a welt and a reminder that pain is undefeated.

You don't forget that feeling.

You don't forget the sting.

You don't forget how fast complacency punishes you.

The instructors loved repeating the same line: "Pain retains." They weren't wrong.

The village itself felt alive.

Each building had quirks you didn't notice until they punished you. A doorway positioned just a little off center. A wall that created a blind angle. A stairwell that forced you to commit before you were ready.

It was psychological warfare disguised as architecture.

There were days we'd run the same structure ten times and still find new ways to screw it up. One day I got turned around so badly I ended up backtracking into a room I'd already cleared. The role player in there just stared at me like, "Really?"

Really.

But that was the point. The village existed to expose every flaw you tried to hide from yourself.

Slowly, painfully, we learned that forward momentum solves more problems than hesitation does.

Move with purpose.

Commit to the corner.

Make the callout.

Fix mistakes at speed.

That was the gospel.

And somewhere in the middle of all that chaos—of sweat and dust and the emotional whiplash of mistake → correction → mistake → correction—we started to change.

We weren't good. Not yet. But we were becoming dangerous to our old selves.

There's a moment in every skill climb where you stop being confused and start being aware. Not competent—aware. That's more important.

Awareness is the doorway to capability.

Night shoots were a whole different religion.

You think you understand darkness until you're standing in an open desert under a moonless sky with nothing but a rifle, a headlamp you're not allowed to use, and a team who's trusting you not to trip over your own feet.

The first time we ran the village at night, the instructors didn't say much. They didn't have to. The silence was instruction.

Everything becomes louder in the dark.

Your breathing.

Your heartbeat.

Your thoughts.

The crunch of gravel under boots.

The metallic click of a safety selector.

Even fear has a sound when the lights are gone.

We moved slower, tighter, more deliberate. Every room felt twice its size. Every corner felt like a coin flip between "clear" and "consequence."

There's something psychological about darkness that daylight kindness hides. In the dark, you lose the illusion of control.

And that's when real learning begins.

One moment from that night is burned into my memory.

We were clearing a long hallway. The kind you see in training videos—narrow, unforgiving, and built to test judgment more than aim. Jarrod was behind me, and even without looking, I could feel his presence like a pressure on my spine.

Halfway down the hall, a role player popped out from a doorway on my left. I didn't see him. I *felt* movement. Some instinct fired before thought could arrive, and I snapped to the threat, muzzle up, command out.

It was sloppy. Late. But it was there.

The instructor's voice—low, approving—came from behind us: "Good. You're starting to see without seeing."

That line changed something in me.

Night became a teacher.

Then came the smoke drills.

If you've never been in an enclosed space filled with training smoke, imagine living inside a fog machine that hates you. Visibility drops to zero. Your lungs burn. Every step feels like moving through wet cement.

But the real enemy isn't the smoke—it's the claustrophobia.

The first time I entered a smoke-filled room, I hesitated just a fraction, and that fraction became failure.

The team flowed past, and I got swallowed by the haze.

When I finally fought my way through, one of the instructors pulled me aside.

"You can't think in there," he said. "Thinking gets you killed. You act. You trust your reps. You trust your team."

Trust your team.

That idea kept coming back, again and again, through every evolution. Not because it sounded good, but because it was survival.

The instructors didn't care how fast you were alone. They cared how reliable you were together.

A good solo run meant nothing. A good team run meant everything.

And slowly, the village started punishing us less. Not because it got easier—but because we stopped fighting it.

We stopped trying to outsmart the maze.

We stopped trying to be heroes.

We stopped trying to perform.

We started doing the job.

That's the shift nobody warns you about—the moment you stop learning the mechanics and start learning the mindset.

Mindset is heavier than any kit you'll ever wear.

One of the biggest lessons came on a day so hot the dust felt like it was cooking from the ground up.

We were doing multi-room clears—big team, full flow, no breaks between runs.

Halfway through a scenario, I hit a wall. Not a real wall—a psychological one.

My brain lagged half a second behind my body. Corners felt too sharp. My feet felt too slow. The village felt like it had grown an extra room just to mess with me.

After the run, I leaned against the container wall, gasping, drenched, cooked from the inside out.

Jarrod walked over, looked at me for a long second, and said:

"Breathe. Then go again."

Not a pep talk. Not a lecture. Not some motivational poster bullshit. Just direction.

So I breathed. And I went again.

And the next run? Better.

That became a theme:

You hit the wall.

You breathe.

You go again.

The simple things always outlast the complicated ones.

Another moment that stuck with me came during a stairwell scenario.

37

Stairs are where judgment goes to die. Every angle is bad. Every elevation change is a liability. Every step is a chance to screw the whole team.

On one run, I hesitated at the top step. Not long. Half a second. Maybe less. But the stack behind me collapsed.

Afterwards, the instructor walked up, didn't raise his voice, didn't scold, didn't humiliate. He just said:

"Your hesitation is louder than your commands."

That line hit like a freight train.

Because he wasn't talking about stairs. He was talking about life.

How many places had I hesitated outside the village?

How many moments had I stalled or second-guessed when someone needed me to be decisive?

How many times have politeness, fear, or overthinking cost momentum?

That stairwell became a mirror.

Later that day, the instructor made me run that exact scenario five more times. I hated him. Then I loved him. Then I hated him again.

But run after run, the hesitation died. Not because I willed it away—but because muscle memory replaced fear with familiarity.

Reps kill fear.

And the instructors weren't shy about adding pressure. If you thought you were getting comfortable, they'd throw in a curveball—a new angle, a screaming role player, a second door you didn't see, or a step that forced you to break your rhythm.

They wanted you uncomfortable, not suffering—learning.

The kind of learning you don't get from books. The kind that stains your shirt and sticks under your fingernails. The kind that comes with bruises in the shapes of lessons.

The village was a teacher with no patience for ego.

But it respected effort.

By the fourth or fifth weekend, something unexpected happened.

We started to click.

Not perfectly. Not consistently. But moments—the kind the instructors called "flashes." A clean slice of a corner. A perfectly timed callout. A room cleared so fluidly it felt choreographed even though it was chaos managed through trust.

Those flashes were fuel.

They told us: "You're not good yet. But you're getting there."

And getting there is addictive.

Addiction is a weird word for something that looks like exhaustion from the outside.

But that's what it became.

We weren't chasing adrenaline. We were chasing clarity—the kind that only shows up when you push yourself to the edge of what you think you can do, fail, and then realize you're still standing.

One of the instructors said it best: "Most people quit when they get tired. Winners quit when they're done."

I wasn't a winner yet. But I started to understand the difference.

Then came the car fire.

Yes, a car fire.

The Marauders training ground had an old beat-up sedan they used for vehicle extractions and approach drills. That day, someone decided to add a smoke generator to "increase realism."

Realism increased.

We were stacking on the driver's side, prepping to pull a role player out. As soon as the smoke kicked on, it mixed with desert heat, dust, and the ungodly scent of burning plastic.

Halfway through the drill, the engine compartment actually ignited. Like, real flames. Not dramatic explosion flames—more like "your HOA is going to fine you" flames.

Everyone froze for half a second because nobody knew if it was planned.

The instructors didn't miss a beat.

"LET IT BURN! ADDS REALISM!"

I swear to God that's what they yelled.

So, we kept going.

Smoke pouring out. Flames licking the hood. Role player screaming. Dust swirling like a curse. It was borderline biblical.

Jarrod pulled the "injured civilian" out through the backseat while I provided cover. My eyes were watering. My throat felt like it had been sandpapered. My brain was doing the math: *Are we really ignoring a car fire right now? *

Yes. Yes we were.

After the drill, one of the instructors sprayed the engine with a fire extinguisher, shrugged, and said, "Well... it'll still run."

It did not still run.

But we learned.

That day taught us what chaos actually feels like—not staged chaos, not theoretical chaos, but the real-world kind that doesn't wait for you to be ready.

And buried inside that chaos was a truth: you don't rise under pressure. You fall to your last good rep.

Our reps were finally starting to matter.

Another evolution that burned itself into memory came during a hostage scenario.

The setup was simple. A role player inside a container. Low light. One entrance. Hostage screaming.

Shooter hiding behind them.

Simple is a lie.

Everything about hostage scenarios is designed to overwhelm you. The noise. The unpredictability. The pressure to choose correctly under conditions that make correctness almost impossible.

I was third in the stack, which meant I was the one expected to make the decisive shot if it opened.

The door flew open.

Screaming. Movement. Hostage flailing. Role player behind them shifting like a shadow with intention.

For a split second, everything in my brain said, *Don't shoot. Don't screw this up*.

That split second was my failure.

The instructor stopped the drill, walked up, and said, "You're thinking again. Thinking is slow. Sight picture. Decision. That's it."

I made the shot clean on the second run.

But the lesson wasn't about accuracy—it was about commitment.

Hesitation is just fear wearing manners.

The instructors kept drilling that into us—not because they wanted robots, but because real-world scenarios don't wait for polite, careful men to find their courage.

You act, or you lose.

One of the more chaotic days involved a rotating-door scenario. The build team had installed a door that opened both ways for the sole purpose of ruining our lives.

The first time I hit it, I pushed instead of pulled, stumbled forward, and jammed the entire stack behind me. Jarrod crashed into my back. The guy behind him crashed into his. It looked like a tactical conga line of failure.

The instructor didn't yell. He just shook his head and said, "Congratulations. You just died creatively."

We ran it again. And again. And again. Each time adjusting micro-movements. Hand placement.

42

Footwork. Communication.

On the tenth run, it clicked. The door moved the right way. The entry flowed. The corners were sliced.

The role player didn't get to shoot anyone.

Progress through pain.

As the weeks went on, the village felt less like an enemy and more like a sparring partner. Still mean.

Still unpredictable. Still built to break you. But fair in its own twisted way.

If you respected it, it taught you.

If you rushed it, it punished you.

If you thought you had it mastered, it reminded you that mastery is a myth.

No matter how confident we felt walking in, the village always found something new to expose.

One day it was angles.

One day it was timing.

One day it was communication.

One day it was emotional control.

One day it was physical exhaustion.

The village was a mirror—one that didn't care about your ego, your excuses, or your good intentions.

But somewhere in all that smoke, dust, sweat, and bruising repetition, something else started to take shape.

We stopped trying to win the village.

We started trying to work with each other.

Teams aren't born from success. They're born from shared failure.

And we were failing together beautifully.

The instructors could see it. Their critiques changed. Less fundamental. More refined. Less "what the hell are you doing?" and more "you're six inches off; fix it."

That was the first sign we weren't beginners anymore.

We weren't good. But we were in the game.

Night movement returned toward the end of the training cycle, and this time the instructors added a twist: dead radios.

"Your comms are down. Figure it out."

Great.

If darkness exposes fear, silence exposes everything else.

We moved as a single organism—slow, deliberate, trying to communicate through taps, squeezes, and intuition. Every shadow felt alive. Every corner felt personal. Every step felt like a dare.

Halfway through the run, I felt something shift internally.

Not fear.

Not adrenaline.

Something quieter.

44

Trust.

The kind you don't announce. The kind you don't brag about.
The kind that shows up when your world shrinks to two feet
of visibility and the only thing keeping you grounded is the
guy behind you.

I wasn't thinking about angles or footwork or getting shot.

I was thinking: *Don't fail the team*.

That was new.

That night, the village became something else.

Not an obstacle. Not a threat. Not a maze designed to
embarrass us.

It became a proving ground.

There's a moment in every difficult pursuit—physical,
emotional, spiritual—where the environment doesn't change,
but you do. The variables stay the same, but your relationship
to them shifts. The fear is still there, but it loses its authority.

That night was that pivot.

We hit our final room, cleared it clean, and the instructor
stepped in behind us, nodding.

"That," he said quietly, "is a team."

No applause. No celebration. No cinematic chorus.

Just acknowledgment.

And that was enough.

The thing about Marauders was that no single drill, no single
moment, no single weekend made the difference. It was the

accumulation. The layering. The slow erosion of old habits, old fears, old stories about who you were and what you were capable of.

The village didn't care about who you thought you were; it cared about who you were becoming.

And becoming is messy.

That's something nobody tells you. Self-transformation looks heroic in hindsight but humiliating in real time. It looks like missing doors, jamming hallways, tripping over your own sling, breathing so hard you sound like you're auditioning for a horror movie, and hoping the role player yelling at you doesn't recognize your panic.

But somewhere in that mess, competence started forming.

Not the sexy, movie version.

The real version—the kind built from reps, sweat, mistakes, corrections, and accountability.

We didn't realize it then, but every weekend was preparing us for something bigger. Something we were nowhere near ready for, even though we thought we were.

SpecOps was coming.

And the village?

The village was the doorway.

You don't know a doorway when you're standing in front of it. You only recognize it after you've walked through and look back at what got stripped away.

The village stripped away a lot.

Politeness.

Hesitation.

Self-doubt disguised as caution.

Performance disguised as competence.

Comfort disguised as readiness.

All of it burned off in that maze.

There was one more moment—small, forgettable to anyone else—that cemented how far we'd come.

It happened on a three-man run.

We moved through the first room clean. Hit the hallway. Flowed left. Sliced the far corner. Started our entry into the next structure.

Halfway through the door, I felt Jarrod's hand press against my back—firm, intentional, corrective.

I shifted.

He filled the gap.

The third man flowed behind us.

We cleared the room like we'd rehearsed it a thousand times.

When we exited the structure, the instructor was standing there with his arms crossed.

He didn't say "Good job."

He didn't say "Clean run."

He didn't even nod.

He just said, "About time."

And somehow, that meant more than any compliment.

You don't notice growth when you're in it. You're too close.
Too tired. Too covered in dust and sweat and frustration to
recognize what's actually changing.

But the instructors weren't looking at our mistakes
anymore—they were looking at our margins. Our edges. The
places where small improvements had compound effects.

They started nitpicking in different ways.

Not "You're doing it wrong."

But "You did it right—now do it faster."

Not "That was sloppy."

But "Your timing was a quarter-second late; fix that."

When someone shifts from correcting failures to refining
details, that's the moment you know you're not in the shallow
end anymore.

By the end of that cycle, the village felt familiar—not
comfortable, not safe, but knowable.

We knew the doors.

We knew the angles.

We knew the traps.

We knew ourselves.

And ourselves were a problem worth fixing.

The final day of that block, the instructors gathered us under
the shade of a warped metal awning that offered mercy only
in theory.

The lead instructor said, "Everything you've seen so far? That was kindergarten."

We laughed.

He didn't.

"You think you've worked hard," he continued. "You think you've pushed yourselves. But you haven't even started yet."

He let that sit in the air like a dare.

"You're going to want to quit next weekend. Most of you won't say it out loud. But you'll feel it. And that's when it gets real."

He was right.

We thought the village was the threshold.

SpecOps was the threshold.

We didn't know it yet, but everything we'd done—every bruise, every mistake, every moment of embarrassment, every small flash of competence, every hit from a UTM round, every doorway we'd misjudged—was the runway leading to the next evolution.

The village was the place where we learned how little we knew.

SpecOps would be the place we learned how far we could go.

But standing there on that final day, sun baking the metal above us, dust settling on our boots like a second skin, something else became clear:

Walking through doors teaches you something.

Walking through *yourself* teaches you more.

Marauders wasn't about tactics.

It was about truth.

And the thing about truth?

It doesn't care how uncomfortable it makes you.

Truth shows up in stress.

It shows up when you're tired, when you're unsure, when the plan breaks down, when the hallway is too tight, when the smoke blinds you, when the role player screams something that spikes your heart rate, when the instructor watches your hesitation like a surgeon studying a tumor.

Truth shows up when you don't have the luxury of pretending.

And if there's one thing Marauders did perfectly, it was stripping away pretense.

By the time we finished that phase, we weren't the same men who walked into the village weeks earlier. We weren't elite. We weren't warriors. We weren't suddenly transformed into something special.

But we were honest.

Honest about our weaknesses.

Honest about our hesitation.

Honest about our fear.

Honest about our gaps.

Honest about what needed fixing.

Honest about who we actually were—not who we imagined ourselves to be.

That honesty?

That was the doorway.

People think transformation is a grand moment. A cinematic epiphany. A sudden lightning strike of clarity.

But it's not.

Transformation is slow erosion.

It's the dust that sticks to you.

The bruise that makes you adjust your stance.

The instructor's voice that echoes in your thoughts.

The repetition that reshapes your instincts.

The embarrassment that teaches you humility.

The small victories that teach you possibility.

It happens quietly.

Incrementally.

Reluctantly.

And then one day, you realize you're not hesitating at the top of the stairwell anymore.

You're moving.

Decisively.

Not because you got braver—but because the fear lost its grip.

The village beat that out of us.

Or maybe it beat it *into* us.

Hard to say the difference.

On the drive home after that final village weekend, I stared out the window at the desert—endless, empty, burning gold in the late afternoon sun. My shirt was soaked. My shoulders were wrecked. My knees felt like borrowed equipment one size too small.

But I wasn't thinking about pain.

I was thinking about what came next.

SpecOps was the first time we'd be pushed past discomfort into actual collapse.

And something in me—quiet, unfamiliar, almost unwelcome—wanted to meet that challenge head-on.

The desert rolled by.

The sky shifted from gold to orange to the first hint of night.

Jarrod drove in silence.

And for the first time since we started this wild journey, I realized something:

I wanted the next doorway.

Even if it led somewhere I wasn't ready for.

Doors had become a metaphor for everything.

Every drill, every rep, every miserable hot Saturday came down to the same simple truth:

You don't get to see what's on the other side until you commit to going through.

Most people stand at the threshold their whole lives.

They peek.

They analyze.

They bargain.

They wait.

We did that too — at first.

But the village beat hesitation out of us one doorway at a time.

I didn't understand the full weight of that lesson until months later. But the foundations were poured here, in this maze of plywood, steel, and sunburn.

Every time we walked into the village, we walked into a different version of ourselves:

One that was still learning.

One that was still failing.

One that was still afraid.

One that was still growing.

We didn't know it, but we were training a new identity — one doorway, one corner, one breath at a time.

There was another moment — small but unforgettable — where the instructors changed the script on us entirely.

It wasn't during a run.

It wasn't during a drill.

It wasn't even during a break.

It happened while we were loading mags.

We were sitting on cracked plastic chairs under a ripped canopy that pretended to offer shade. Dust stuck to everything — sweat, skin, ammo boxes, rifles resting against our shins like tired animals.

The instructor walked over, grabbed a mag from my table without asking, held it up, and said:

"This is your life. One round at a time. Don't waste them."

He wasn't talking about ammo.

He walked away before any of us could process it.

Jarrod and I looked at each other.

He shrugged.

But I knew exactly what the instructor meant.

Every rep was a round.

Every moment of hesitation was a round.

Every mistake was a round.

Every lesson was a round.

What you put in the mag is what you bring to the fight — literal or metaphorical.

The village wasn't teaching tactics.

It was teaching stewardship.

Of attention.

Of effort.

Of fear.

Of the space between impulse and action.

Every run was a choice:

Fill the mag with intent, or dump trash into it and pretend it's the same thing.

It wasn't.

Later that same day, we ran one of the most chaotic drills in the entire cycle.

They called it "Doors to Nowhere."

The build team had reconfigured the village overnight — added walls, blocked passages, flipped entire layouts just to break our pattern recognition. Nothing was where it had been. Nothing worked the way we expected.

The first time we ran it, we got lost.

Not metaphorically. Literally.

Full team. Full kit. Full confusion.

We breached the first doorway clean. Entered the second structure. Took a hard left. Opened a door... and found another door. Opened that one... and ran straight into a wall.

A dead end.

A room with no exit.

A doorway to absolutely nowhere.

Behind us, the instructor said, "Good. Figure it out."

So we backed up, regrouped, and tried the next door.

That one led to a crooked hallway that looped around in a U-shape and spit us back into the room we'd just cleared.

We were rats in a maze. Tactical, sweaty rats.

The third door looked promising — until it led us into a room with two doors, one locked and one open.

We chose the open one. Wrong choice. Another dead end.

"THINK!" the instructor shouted. "Use your fucking BRAIN!"

We were thinking. Thinking too much.

And that was the problem.

When you overthink, you lose tempo. When you lose tempo, the village eats you alive.

On the fourth attempt, something changed.

Not the layout.

Not the walls.

Not the doors.

Us.

We stopped trying to predict the maze.

We stopped trying to be smart.

We stopped trying to "beat" the design.

We started flowing.

Room.

Corner.

Threshold.

Door.

Door.

Door.

Move.

Move.

Move.

We took the path the village gave us instead of the path we wanted.

And suddenly — the labyrinth opened.

We found the exit.

We hit the final room.

We cleared it clean.

The instructor stepped inside, looked at the team, and said:

"That's what happens when you stop fighting the environment."

He wasn't talking about the village.

He was talking about life.

That drill stayed with me.

Because "Doors to Nowhere" wasn't just a training exercise —
it was a metaphor disguised as plywood.

How many times in life do we:

Pick the obvious door?

Pick the easy door?

Pick the familiar door?

Pick the door that used to work?

Pick the door that *should* work?

Pick the door that feels safe?

Only to find...

A wall.

A dead end.

A trap.

A loop back into the same room we swore we'd left behind.

The village was honest in ways life often isn't.

Most doorways in life lie to you.

These didn't.

If a door led nowhere, it told you the truth immediately.

You just had to be willing to see it.

Weeks later, I caught myself navigating a stressful moment in
real life — a moment where I wanted to force a situation,
push a conversation, argue my way through a problem.

And the memory hit me:

"Stop fighting the environment."

Sometimes the only way forward is through the door you
didn't want, at the angle you didn't expect, with the
humility you didn't know you needed.

The village taught that through repetition, frustration, and a
maze that didn't care about my opinions.

One of the instructors summed it up perfectly:

"This place doesn't want you to win. It wants you to learn."

We learned.

Not gracefully. Not quickly. Not without bruises.

But we learned.

By the end of that day, every one of us had sweat-soaked
vests, bruised forearms, raw knuckles, and a level of fatigue
that lived somewhere behind the eyes.

But we also had something we didn't have before:

Trust.

Not trust in ourselves — that would come later.

Trust in each other.

The village took us apart individually.

Then it put us back together collectively.

Piece by piece.

Corner by corner.

Door by miserable door.

You don't build a team through comfort.

You build a team through shared confusion resolved at speed.

And by the time we finished that final village evolution, something had changed in the air around us.

We weren't moving like individuals anymore.

We weren't thinking like strangers.

We weren't surviving on luck.

We were operating.

Not perfectly.

Not professionally.

Not cleanly.

But *together*.

There was one final moment — tiny, almost invisible — that showed just how far we'd come.

It happened during a simple two-room flow drill. No smoke. No screaming. No dead radios. No maze.

Just fundamentals.

We hit the first room clean.

Then the second.

As we exited, the instructor stood outside the doorway, arms folded, sunglasses hiding whatever judgment was brewing behind them.

He pointed at us one by one and said:

"You. Finally using your legs."

"You. Good muzzle discipline."

"You. Stop breathing so loud."

"You. Don't know what you did, but it worked."

And then he pointed at me.

"You... are slightly less terrible."

It was the highest praise I'd ever received.

We laughed — exhausted, delirious, covered in dust and ego shrapnel. But beneath the humor was pride. Earned pride. Not the performative kind you post online. The quiet kind you feel when you look at your own progress and think:

I'm not who I was.

That's what the village gave us.

Not perfection.

Not mastery.

Not swagger.

Progress.

Progress is built from discomfort, confusion, humility, and the relentless willingness to go again.

On the last day of the block, as we packed up our gear and loaded our rifles into the truck, Jarrod looked at me and said:

"We survived."

He meant it as a joke.

But he wasn't wrong.

We had survived the village.

And the village, in its own brutal way, had prepared us for what came next.

SpecOps.

The chapter we weren't ready for.

The chapter we thought we understood.

The chapter that would take everything the village taught us... and multiply it by ten.

But standing there in the fading desert heat, dust swirling around our feet like a closing curtain, one truth settled into place:

You don't get to choose your trial by fire.

But you do get to choose whether you walk through the door.

And we were ready for another door.

Even if it led to hell.

Hell wasn't a metaphor.

Hell had a schedule.

And the instructors handed it to us with the kind of grin that told you they'd been waiting all month to watch us meet it.

Before we even left the village for the final time, the lead instructor called us into a loose semicircle.

Dust swirled around his boots. His sunglasses were so scratched they looked frosted. His voice cut through the heat like a blade.

"You boys think you've done something."

Not a question. A statement.

"You think because you can slice a corner without pointing your gun at your buddy, you're hot shit."

We stayed quiet.

"You think because you made it through a smoke run without crying, you're operators."

Silence again.

He let it stretch.

Then he said the line that would haunt the next chapter of our lives:

"Next weekend, the village is gone. The breaks are gone. The shade is gone. The mercy is gone."

He paced in front of us slowly, like a man inspecting cattle before an auction.

"SpecOps is the point where most people quit. They don't quit out loud—they quit inside. They quit quietly. They quit where no one can see it. And then they go through the motions and pretend they're fine."

He stopped walking.

"Don't be that man."

Every one of us felt that in our bones.

"This was the warm-up," he continued. "The real work starts now. The real failure starts now. The real

growth starts now."

He pointed at the village behind us.

"This place taught you doors. Next weekend teaches you walls."

We didn't know what he meant.

Not yet.

But we would.

By the time he finished the briefing, the sun was low over the horizon, cutting long shadows across the container walls. The air felt heavy. Like it knew what was coming.

Jarrod nudged me with his elbow.

"You ready for whatever the hell that means?"

"Nope."

"Same."

We both laughed. But it wasn't the easy laughter from earlier weeks. It was tighter. Sharper. The kind you use when you're bracing for impact but pretending you're not.

As we threw our bags into the truck and slammed the tailgate shut, something occurred to me:

The village had been a grind.

A puzzle.

A teacher.

A mirror.

A sparring partner.

But it had also been a comfort.

As brutal as it was, it was familiar brutality.

Next weekend?

There would be no familiarity.

We were stepping into the unknown.

The unknown has weight.

It sits on your chest. It tightens your breath. It makes everything quieter — not peaceful quiet, but the kind of quiet that feels like a pressure drop before a storm.

Driving away from the village that evening, I stared out at the open desert — the same stretch of land that had become our proving ground week after week. But for the first time, it didn't feel like the end of something.

It felt like the beginning of something worse.

The desert has a way of telling the truth. It strips away comfort, cosmetic courage, and whatever bullshit stories you tell yourself about who you are. There's nowhere to hide in a place where even the air feels honest.

And that night, the desert whispered the same sentence over and over:

"You're not ready."

It wasn't an insult. It was a warning.

SpecOps wasn't going to test our skills.

It was going to test our identity.

There's a difference.

Skills you can practice.

Identity gets revealed.

Jarrod must've felt it too because halfway home he broke the long silence with a question that wasn't a question, "You think we're walking into something we can walk back out of?"

I didn't answer right away.

Finally, I said, "I think we're walking into something that's going to change us."

He nodded once — slow, grounded — the kind of nod that says, *Yeah. I feel that too*.

We rode the rest of the way in silence.

Not fear.

Not dread.

Not even anticipation.

Something deeper.

The awareness that we were stepping into a chapter we didn't control.

The village had shown us who we were.

SpecOps would show us who we weren't.

Those are two different doorways. And the second one is always harder to walk through.

When I got home that night, I dropped my gear on the floor and collapsed onto the edge of the bed.

My legs felt like wet rope. My shoulders felt like they had been borrowed from a mannequin. Every inch of my body had something to complain about.

But my mind?

My mind was awake.

Alert.

Alive.

Scanning for something it couldn't name.

I replayed the village in my head — the doors, the corners, the runs, the breathless moments, the instructor's critiques, the laughs, the failures, the little bursts of competence.

I tried to use those memories as reassurance.

They didn't help.

Because deep down, I knew the truth:

Nothing we had done was going to prepare us for what came next.

SpecOps wasn't the next step.

It was the cliff.

And we were already leaning over the edge.

Sleep didn't come easy that night.

My body wanted it. My brain refused.

Every time I closed my eyes, I saw doorways—some open, some closed, some leading into darkness, some leading back into the same damn room I'd just escaped.

My mind kept replaying the instructor's words:

"This was kindergarten."

If that was kindergarten, then what the hell was coming next?

At some point, exhaustion won. But it wasn't restful sleep—it was the kind where your mind keeps running drills even in the dark. I dreamt of stairwells. Of smoke. Of the sound of my own heartbeat echoing in a container hallway. Of Jarrod's hand on my back guiding me through a doorway I didn't want to enter.

Morning didn't feel like morning. It felt like a continuation.

Coffee tasted burned. My hands were still shaking slightly from the adrenaline hangover. My gear sat in a pile by the wall like a sleeping animal waiting to be woken up and unleashed again.

I packed it anyway.

Because even though fear was building, something else was growing right beside it:

Resolve.

Fear tells you what might happen.

Resolve tells you what you're going to do anyway.

SpecOps wasn't optional.

Not for us.

Not anymore.

We had started something in that village—something raw, something uncomfortable, something that

felt bigger than bruises and sweat and tactical movement.

The village had exposed our weaknesses.

SpecOps would expose our limits.

And exposure is where transformation happens.

Driving to training the next weekend felt different.

The sun was brighter.

The air felt sharper.

Even the road seemed to stretch longer, like the desert was putting distance between who we had been and who we were about to become.

Jarrod was quiet. Focused. Not his usual cracking-jokes-to-kill-the-tension self.

At one point he said, "My stomach's doing that rollercoaster drop thing."

"Mine too," I said.

"Good. Means we're alive."

He wasn't wrong.

When we turned onto the dirt road leading toward the range, the entire world seemed to still.

No breeze. No birds. Just heat and gravity.

It felt like approaching a threshold.

Because it was.

The village had its own energy—chaotic, disorienting, frustrating, punishing.

SpecOps had a different one.

It didn't feel chaotic.

It felt inevitable.

Like walking into a storm that had been waiting for you specifically.

Like stepping into a chapter that already had your name written in it.

Like the moment before a door blows open—not the hit, not the entry, but the breath right before.

That moment where everything is possible and nothing is guaranteed.

We parked.

We stepped out.

Dust rose around our boots.

And without saying a word, we both knew:

This was where the next version of us would be forged—or broken.

Forging sounds noble.

It isn't.

Forging is heat, pressure, and the violent removal of anything that doesn't belong.

And that's exactly what waited for us.

But before SpecOps truly began, before the beatdowns and
the breakthroughs, before the suffering and the strange
moments of clarity that only show up when you're
half-delirious, something else happened that shifted the tone
completely.

It was small.

It was quiet.

It was easy to miss.

But it mattered.

As the group started gathering near the staging area, the lead
instructor walked past us. Same scratched sunglasses. Same
no-nonsense gait. Same expression that told you he could see
through your confidence like glass.

He stopped. Looked at the two of us.

Then said, almost casually:

"You boys showed up."

He didn't smile.

He didn't soften.

He just said it like a fact.

Then he walked away.

Three words.

Zero drama.

All impact.

71

"You boys showed up."

It wasn't praise.

It was acknowledgment.

And acknowledgment is rarer than compliments.

Compliments tell you someone likes what you did.

Acknowledgment tells you someone sees who you are.

And in that moment, we weren't the guys who hesitated in stairwells or jammed doorways or got lost in container mazes.

We were the guys who came back.

Who didn't fold.

Who didn't ghost the training.

Who didn't pretend we were fine when we weren't.

Who didn't hide behind excuses.

We showed up.

Even when we were tired.

Even when we were embarrassed.

Even when the village kicked our ass.

Even when the next evolution terrified us.

We showed up.

And showing up is the first test of every man who wants to grow.

SpecOps would be the second.

The instructors called us into formation. Dust swirled. The air felt like a held breath.

"Listen up," the lead instructor said. "What happens today will stay with you for the rest of your life."

He wasn't being dramatic.

He was being accurate.

"You will hate me at some point," he continued. "You will doubt yourselves. You will think about quitting. Some of you will wish you'd stayed home."

He let the silence settle.

"Good. That means you're in the right place."

Then he gave the command.

"Mask up."

The world changed instantly.

When the mask seals, the world becomes smaller.

Your vision narrows.

Your breath becomes louder.

Your awareness collapses inward.

You stop thinking in sentences and start thinking in impulses.

The instructors knew exactly what they were doing.

Masks aren't just about protecting your face from UTM rounds.

Masks are about stripping away comfort.

They turn the world into a tunnel.

They make your own breath sound like an enemy.

They trap heat against your skin.

They fog, they suffocate, they amplify every insecurity you didn't know you had.

And once the mask goes on, there's only one thought left:

Don't fail.

The lead instructor walked down the line slowly, tapping each one of us on the shoulder with the same gloved hand that had hammered us for weeks.

"You're going to find yourself today," he said. "Or you're going to find your breaking point. Sometimes they're the same thing."

Jarrod stood to my right. I could hear his breathing through the mask — sharp, controlled, present.

My own breath sounded like a drum inside my skull.

The instructor raised his hand.

The sun was behind him, turning his silhouette into something mythic — a dark outline holding all the power in the world.

Then he dropped his hand.

"GO!"

Chaos detonated.

UTM rounds cracked.

Voices shouted.

Dust exploded upward as boots slammed the earth.

The world became noise, heat, and instinct.

We sprinted toward the first structure — a long container with a doorway that always felt too small for entry at speed.

My heart hammered like it was trying to break out of my chest. Not fear — readiness.

Mask breathing is different. It forces you to fight yourself. Every inhale feels like you're pulling air through a straw. Every exhale fogs the lenses. Every movement reminds you that you're sealed inside your own limitations.

We stacked on the door.

Jarrod on point.

Me behind him.

Another teammate anchoring.

The instructor screamed: "MOVE!"

Jarrod hit the doorway first — clean, aggressive, slicing the near corner like he'd been born doing it.

I flowed in behind him.

The room was dim. Hot. Crowded with shapes that might have been furniture or obstacles or just the ghosts of bad decisions.

The role player — masked, armed, and far too enthusiastic about his job — popped up from behind a barrier and fired.

UTM rounds snapped past my ear like angry bees.

I hugged the wall, turned, and returned fire. Markers splattered across the target's vest. He went down dramatically, like he wanted an Oscar for "Best Death in a Low-Budget Action Sequence."

We cleared the room.

"NEXT!"

We moved.

The next doorway loomed ahead — darker, narrower, filled with the unknown.

I could feel my legs start to shake. Not from fatigue — from adrenaline so thick it felt electric.

Masks do that.

Masks make you confront a version of yourself you can't negotiate with.

They remove comfort.

They remove expression.

They remove oxygen just fast enough to make doubt louder.

Every fear you managed to shove down during normal training tries to claw its way back up.

But there was no time for fear.

We hit the next threshold with the kind of momentum that came from weeks of failure welded into instinct. Jarrod flowed right. I flowed left. Our third man pushed down the center.

A role player burst out of a closet-sized space like a jack-in-the-box loaded with malice. He fired a burst of UTM rounds directly into my shoulder.

Pain detonated.

UTM rounds hurt through a plate carrier — sharp, stinging, humiliating pain. Pain that makes your vision blink. Pain that makes your brain hesitate.

I didn't hesitate.

Pain wasn't new anymore.

Pain was information.

Pain was feedback.

Pain was a cue.

I pushed forward, returned fire, and dropped the threat.

Jarrod shouted a command I couldn't make out through the mask. It didn't matter. I knew what he meant. That was the thing about training with someone long enough: words become optional.

We cleared the room.

"NEXT!"

We moved again.

My breathing was getting heavier now — mask heat building, sweat pooling, UTM impacts lighting up my nerves like static electricity. But something else was happening underneath all that:

77

Clarity.

The kind that comes only when everything unnecessary gets stripped away.

No thoughts.

No ego.

No over-analysis.

Just movement.

Just presence.

Just the next door.

The next structure was a nightmare — the kind the instructors built when they were either bored or in a creative mood with malicious intent.

Narrow entry.

Blind corner.

Immediate threat zone.

Zero forgiveness.

Jarrod hit the doorframe, moved left.

I flowed behind him.

A role player screamed something incoherent and charged from the far corner — too fast, too loud, too aggressive.

"CONTACT!"

I fired three rounds center mass.

He stumbled.

But he kept coming.

Second role player behind him.

Then a hostage being dragged.

My brain tried to think.

Masks don't let you think.

Sight picture.

Threat.

Decision.

Action.

That's all there is.

I waited for the half-second window — the hostage shifted, the threat exposed an inch too much of his torso — and I took the shot.

Clean hit.

Hostage dropped to the ground, covering their ears.

Role player went down like his contract required dramatic flair.

We secured the room.

By now my lungs were on fire.

Every inhale felt like breathing through a furnace filter. Every exhale fogged the mask until the world turned into a smeared hallucination of shapes, shadows, and instinct. Sweat pooled under the seal, dripped down my jawline, soaked my shirt.

But I wasn't thinking about any of that.

I was thinking about the next doorway.

Because once you're in motion, stopping isn't an option. Stopping is death. Stopping is doubt.

Stopping is the moment your brain sees an opening to whisper all the things you don't need to hear.

We didn't stop.

"NEXT!"

We moved.

The final structure of the run was the worst one — deliberately designed to break rhythm, break flow, break confidence. A long hallway with offset doorways and staggered angles. A kill zone for anyone who hesitated.

Jarrod entered first.

A role player fired a burst and hit him square in the thigh plate.

He stumbled, but he didn't pause.

He just shouted, "LEFT!" and drove forward.

I filled the space behind him, slicing the opposite corner. A second threat appeared — low crouch, fast movement, firing wild.

I dropped him with two controlled rounds.

Another doorway. Another movement. Another decision made faster than thought allowed.

We were in pure instinct mode — the place the instructors kept pushing us toward, the place where training overrides panic.

Then came the final moment.

A role player stepped into the end of the hallway holding a rifle and a screaming hostage.

Everything in me wanted to freeze.

Everything in me wanted to think.

Everything in me wanted to hesitate.

But weeks in the village had carved that hesitation out of me.

The hostage shifted.

The threat exposed half an inch of chest.

I took the shot.

Clean.

The instructor called: "END EX!"

The world stopped.

Silence crashed into the space like a hammer. My breathing filled the mask. The heat caught up. The pain in my shoulder lit up like a delayed fuse. Jarrod bent over, hands on knees, gasping.

But underneath all that noise, exhaustion, and adrenaline—one truth pulsed:

We didn't break.

Not here.

Not today.

The instructors walked toward us slowly, like judges emerging from the dust.

One of them pointed at us and said:

"That... is what the village was training you for."

Not praise.

Recognition.

Acknowledgment of transformation.

Because transformation doesn't announce itself.

It shows up in moments where you act like the man you've been trying to become.

When we finally pulled our masks off, the air felt cold even though it wasn't.

Fresh air always feels like a gift after you've spent twenty minutes wrestling your own breath inside a sealed piece of plastic.

I wiped sweat from my forehead. Jarrod ripped his mask off with the enthusiasm of a man escaping a hostage situation.

We both looked wrecked — shirts soaked, faces red, eyes wide in that post-adrenaline, "I'm alive but barely" kind of way.

The instructor walked up, looked at us for half a second, and said:

"Good. Now do it again."

Not "great work."

Not "that was solid."

Not even "hydrate."

Just:

Do it again.

And that was the moment I understood the real heart of this entire chapter of training:

Growth doesn't care about your feelings.

Growth doesn't clap for you.

Growth doesn't pause because you're tired.

Growth doesn't reward you for survival.

It demands repetition.

It demands you get back on the line while your lungs still burn.

It demands you pick up the ram while your hands are still shaking.

It demands you enter the next room even though the last one still echoes in your nerves.

The village had taught us how to move.

SpecOps was teaching us how to endure.

And endurance is the birthplace of identity.

The second run was worse.

Not because we failed — but because now we *knew* what was coming.

Anticipation is a heavier weight than ignorance.

Your body braces.

Your mind recoils.

Your breath tightens.

Your confidence wavers.

Your imagination tries to sabotage you.

But we moved anyway.

The second run wasn't clean.

It wasn't pretty.

It wasn't heroic.

But it was committed.

And commitment is what the instructors cared about.

By the end of that second run, we were shaking.

By the end of that second run, we were drenched.

By the end of that second run, we were different men than the ones who started it.

Exhaustion erases pretense.

In exhaustion, you find the truth.

Truth about who you are.

Truth about what you fear.

Truth about what you avoid.

Truth about what you cling to.

Truth about what you're capable of.

And the truth of that day was simple:

We didn't quit.

Not mentally.

Not emotionally.

Not physically.

We stayed in the fight.

Staying in the fight isn't about winning.

Staying in the fight is about refusing to disappear.

Quitting doesn't always look like walking away.

Sometimes it looks like going through the motions.

Sometimes it looks like performing instead of committing.

Sometimes it looks like hesitation dressed up as caution.

Sometimes it looks like silence when you need to speak.

Sometimes it looks like comfort when you need pressure.

But we didn't disappear.

We didn't run from the next door.

We didn't slow the stack.

We didn't ask for mercy.

We didn't let fear vote.

We stayed present.

And presence under pressure is rare.

After the second run ended, the instructors gathered us again. Dust rippled through the air like slow motion. Sweat stung my eyes. My lungs felt overclocked.

The lead instructor looked at all of us — not with pride, not with disappointment, but with something he almost never showed:

Respect.

"Most of you did better than you think," he said. "Most of you did worse than you realize."

He let that contradiction settle.

"That's growth."

He paced slowly, each step deliberate.

"Pain is a truth-teller. Fatigue is a truth-teller. Stress is a truth-teller. When everything hurts and you're still moving, that's who you really are."

Then he pointed at the village in the distance — barely visible through heat shimmer.

"That place taught you how to go through doors."

Then he pointed at the structures behind him.

"This place teaches you why."

He wasn't wrong.

There's a moment in any journey where skill stops being the point. Where tactics stop being the point.

Where physical ability stops being the point.

What remains — the only thing that survives — is character.

Character under fire.

Character under fatigue.

Character under confusion.

Character under impact.

Character under the mask.

SpecOps wasn't a tactics course.

SpecOps was a character course.

And we were only on day one.

We stumbled back to the staging area like men returning from a war they hadn't known they were fighting until it was over.

Masks hung around our necks like defeated helmets.

Rifles sagged across our chests.

Sweat darkened our shirts.

Mud clung to our knees.

Jarrod looked at me and said, "My soul needs electrolytes."

Same.

We dumped empty mags into a pile, reloaded in silence, and waited for whatever fresh hell the instructors had planned next.

But they didn't give us another run.

Instead, the lead instructor stepped forward and said, "That's it for today."

No celebration.

No closure.

No easy exit.

Just an abrupt ending — the kind that leaves you alone with your own thoughts.

We packed our gear in near silence. The only sounds were Velcro tearing, mags clicking, boots crunching on desert gravel, and the occasional pained groan from someone discovering a new bruise.

As we walked toward the truck, the sun started to drop behind the hills, casting the range in that golden, end-of-day light that makes everything feel more dramatic than it really is.

Jarrod and I reached the truck at the same time, dropped our gear in the bed, and leaned against the tailgate like two men who had survived a baptism by fire.

For a long moment, neither of us spoke.

Finally, Jarrod said, "Well... that escalated quickly."

I laughed — or tried to. It came out more like a cough.

"Yeah," I said. "And that was the warm-up."

He nodded, rubbing the impact mark on his thigh plate. "You get tagged pretty bad?"

"Shoulder," I said. "Feels like someone hit me with a baseball bat made of angry."

"Yeah, that tracks."

We stood there for a moment — breathing, processing, decompressing. Not emotionally. Physically.

Our bodies were unloading adrenaline in real time, shaking it out through our fingers, our shoulders, our legs.

Adrenaline is a liar. It convinces you you're fine... until it leaves. Then it hands you the bill.

As the last of the sunlight slipped behind the horizon, I felt something shift inside me. Not dramatic. Not some cinematic epiphany. Something small. Subtle. Almost quiet.

A new awareness.

A new edge.

A new understanding of what doors — literal and metaphorical — actually demand.

It wasn't courage.

It wasn't confidence.

It wasn't pride.

It was commitment.

Commitment to move.

Commitment to decide.

Commitment to act.

Commitment to enter.

Commitment to transform.

Commitment without comfort.

Because comfort is the enemy of growth.

And the village had stripped comfort from us one door at a time.

As we climbed into the truck, Jarrod said, "You think we're ready for next weekend?"

I didn't answer immediately.

Then I said the most honest thing I'd said all day:

"I don't think readiness matters anymore."

He raised an eyebrow. "What does matter?"

"Showing up," I said. "And going through the door anyway."

He nodded once—slow, heavy, understanding.

"Then yeah," he said. "We're ready."

The drive home was quiet.

Not the awkward kind.

Not the exhausted kind.

The reflective kind — the kind where your body is wrecked but your mind is wide awake.

The desert outside the window looked different after SpecOps. The same landscape we had driven through a hundred times now felt like a boundary we had crossed — a physical marker between the men we had been and the men we were becoming.

Jarrod finally broke the silence.

"You know what's messed up?" he said.

"What?"

"I think I liked it."

I didn't even pretend to be surprised.

"Yeah," I said. "Me too."

Because here's the truth no one tells you about hardship: once you push through the first wave of fear, pain, and self-doubt, there's something on the other side that feels... clean.

Not comfortable.

Not easy.

Not pleasurable.

Clean.

Like stripping off an old layer of yourself.

Like rinsing off the bullshit you didn't know you were carrying.

Like discovering something inside you that wasn't dead — just dormant.

SpecOps didn't give us new identities.

It revealed the ones buried under years of convenience and complacency.

The sun kept dropping.

The temperature followed.

The sky shifted from orange to pink to purple to deep desert blue.

Somewhere in that slow transition, I realized something:

The village had been teaching us how to enter doors.

SpecOps was teaching us how to walk out of them different.

We weren't the best.

We weren't the strongest.

We weren't the fastest.

We weren't the most experienced.

But we were willing.

Willing to be uncomfortable.

Willing to be humbled.

Willing to be broken down.

Willing to be rebuilt.

Willing to keep going even when the path was unclear.

Willing to show up.

That's the doorway most men avoid.

Not because they can't open it — but because they're afraid of what they'll see on the other side.

We weren't afraid anymore.

Not because fear vanished — fear never vanishes — but because fear had lost the right to vote.

By the time we pulled into my driveway, the last light of the day had collapsed into darkness.

I grabbed my gear, slung it over my shoulder, and felt every muscle in my body protest.

Jarrod looked at me and smirked.

"See you next weekend?"

"Wouldn't miss it."

And for the first time, I meant it with my whole chest.

Not out of pride.

Not out of bravado.

Not out of ego.

But because I wanted to see what was on the other side of the next door.

There's a moment after every hard evolution — after every beatdown, every drill, every rep that drags you past your comfort zone — where your body is wrecked but your mind sharpens.

It's the paradox of pressure.

Pressure collapses you and clarifies you at the same time.

That night, as I dropped my gear in the hallway and collapsed into a chair, I realized something I hadn't been able to articulate before:

Every door we went through at Marauders...

Every failure...

Every hesitation...

Every correction...

Every run that made us feel like idiots...

Every instructor critique that cut deeper than it sounded...

Every moment we got shot, smoked, confused, lost, or humbled...

All of it was preparation.

Preparation for moments where you don't get to be perfect — you only get to be present.

The village didn't make us skilled.

SpecOps didn't make us tough.

They made us willing.

Willing is a different kind of power.

Skill can fail under pressure.

Strength can fail under fatigue.

Memory can fail under adrenaline.

Ego always fails under truth.

But willingness — the willingness to move forward anyway — that survives.

That endures.

That transforms.

As I sat there replaying the day, I didn't think about the perfect shots.

I didn't think about the clean rooms.

I didn't think about the moments where the instructors nodded.

I thought about the missed corners.

The UTM hits.

The panic under the mask.

The hesitation that almost returned.

The exhaustion that tried to pull me out of myself.

And the fact that none of it stopped me.

The man I had been a few months earlier would've quit quietly.

Would've backed out gracefully.

Would've said he "needed a break."

Would've justified his exit with logic that sounded reasonable.

But that man was gone.

Somewhere between the first door we botched and the last one we cleared, he disappeared.

A newer version was forming — rough, unpolished, inconsistent — but real.

And that version wasn't interested in quitting anymore.

He was interested in becoming.

Becoming isn't glamorous.

Becoming is quiet.

Becoming is slow.

Becoming is painful.

Becoming is repetitive.

Becoming is made of steps so small you don't realize you've moved.

But one day, you look back and realize you're miles from where you started.

SpecOps wasn't the end of that journey — it was the furnace.

The place where the village's lessons got tested under heat.

The place where doors became decisions.

The place where hesitation became memory.

The place where fear became familiar.

The place where we stopped performing and started transforming.

As I finally pushed myself out of the chair, every joint popping in protest, I walked to the bathroom and caught my reflection in the mirror.

I looked wrecked.

Dust-streaked.

Sweat-soaked.

Jaw clenched.

Eyes tired.

But there was something else in my face — something I hadn't seen before.

Presence.

Not confidence.

Not pride.

Not swagger.

Presence.

The calm that shows up when you stop pretending and start participating in your own life.

I didn't smile.

I didn't try to hype myself up.

I didn't rehearse some internal victory speech.

I just nodded once at my reflection — a small, almost involuntary acknowledgment:

You showed up.

Then I turned off the light, walked down the hallway, and collapsed into bed.

My body hurt.

My brain buzzed.

My nerves hummed.

My heart was still somewhere between fear and hunger.

But underneath all that noise, something steady sat in the center of my chest:

Readiness.

Not readiness for skill.

Not readiness for perfection.

Not readiness for glory.

Readiness for whatever the next door demanded.

Because that was the real lesson of the village:

The door doesn't care if you're ready.

It only cares if you enter.

And I was done standing on thresholds.

I didn't know what the next door would hold.

Pain.

Failure.

Breakdown.

Breakthrough.

Maybe all of it.

But I knew this:

Whatever was waiting on the other side, I wouldn't be facing it as the man who walked into the village months ago.

I'd be facing it as the man forged by every door that led nowhere.

Every dead end.

Every wrong turn.

Every failure.

Every hesitation burned out of me in heat and dust and repetition.

Every moment that demanded I move anyway.

The village didn't make me fearless.

It made me honest.

And honesty is the only thing strong enough to push you through the doors that matter.

This chapter of the story doesn't end with a triumph.

It doesn't end with celebration.

It doesn't end with mastery.

It ends with a threshold.

A door in front of me.

A door I can't avoid.

A door I can't predict.

A door I can't prepare for.

A door I will walk through anyway.

Because that's the path.

That's the work.

That's the becoming.

And this time?

There are no doors to nowhere.

Only the door to what comes next.

EVERYTHING EVERYWHERE ALL AT ONCE

They didn't call it an exam, but that's what it felt like—two days where every drill we'd ever done showed up at the same time, wearing boots and a bad attitude.

We staged before sunrise because the sun is the only thing meaner than the instructors. Trucks idled in a loose line like herd animals. Radios hissed. Someone tried to stretch and groaned like an old house in a windstorm. I checked my gear like it was going to develop morals if I stared hard enough. Jarrod caught my eye and gave me that nod guys use when they're about to make a shared mistake on purpose.

The brief was fast and optimistic, like all briefs are before reality hits. Objectives. Sectors. Timeline. The part where someone says, "Minimal sleep," like that's new information. Vehicles were already hot. You could smell diesel and dust and breakfast that wasn't going to happen.

"Load up."

I climbed into the back with too much kit and not enough knees. Door slammed. The world turned into black steel and radio chatter. We weren't playing house anymore. We were Play-Doh shoved through a mold and whatever shape came out was going to have to do.

The first insertion felt like a roller coaster with fewer safety protocols. Vehicle doors blew open and the day exploded. Blank fire popped in bursts—short, staccato corrections to anything soft in your brain. The village was already awake, all plywood teeth and steel bones. Smoke crept like it had a secret. Someone yelled MOVING and everyone else yelled MOVING because repetition is how you borrow courage.

We hit the dirt and spread like we meant it. Breacher team cut left. I took right with Jarrod on my shoulder, our shadows doing a worse job than we were. The heat arrived early—one of those Arizona mornings that feels personal. You breathe and the air complains.

The first structure was simple by design, which means it still tried to kill us. We flowed in, sliced corners, paid attention to hands and eyes and that low hum in your chest that says everything is fine until it isn't. Role-players did their thing—pleading voices, bad decisions, that one guy whose hobby is getting inside your head at inopportune times. We cleared, exhaled, and immediately inhaled new orders.

There wasn't time to feel proud or dumb. Just next.

If you haven't carried the breacher's ram, you have missed a religious experience. The thing weighs what a bad conscience feels like—call it two hundred pounds in the moment, forty-eight later when you're bragging, and precisely whatever number makes your lower back start Googling chiropractors during lunch. We swapped it around like a cursed heirloom. The guy who had it wore that face we all get right before a sneeze or a break-up.

"Hey, man, you look great," I said.

"Liar," he said, and then shouldered it anyway because that's what we do.

By late morning the cadence had settled into a loop: vehicle drops, sprint, stack, breach, clear, reset, water, lie about how much water you need, go again. The radios were a constant weather system—squalls of useful words, high-pressure fronts of static, the occasional lightning bolt of "Say again?" that made everyone glance at their antennas like that would help. Command voices came through clean and calm, and you could feel the calm travel down the line the way panic does when you let it. We were getting better at exporting the right thing.

Midday made everything funny in that borderline delirious way. The tower—our old frenemy—wore a shawl of smoke. That was by design. Wind had opinions. The plan had four legs and we were trying to teach it to fetch. We moved in a cross-town push, bounding between cover like the ground was lava and adulthood was optional. That's when somebody yelled a word you don't yell unless you mean it.

"BLACK! BLACK! BLACK!"

It hit like a spell. The whole op froze. Every team took a knee. Muzzles dropped. Voices shut up. Even the wind seemed to hold its breath.

The red car at the base of the rappelling tower was on fire.

Not fake fire. Not movie fire. Real fire—the kind that licks up into dry air with ambition. One of the pyro pots had rolled where it shouldn't and the heat had found something to love. In a plywood village, that's a plot twist with a short runtime.

We watched it in a synchronized silence that would've been beautiful if it wasn't about to be tragic. A role-player sprinted in from nowhere like a responsible raccoon and started kicking dirt onto the flames with the resigned fury of a man who knows he will be telling this story to his wife without the drama she expects. The instructors scanned the horizon the way men do when they're measuring how much stupid is left.

From my knee I said, not loudly but not to myself either, "Let it burn—adds realism."

Jarrod snorted. Someone near me laughed through their nose like a cartoon horse. The role-player stomped and stomped and then the flames died like they remembered their place. One of the cadre gave a thumbs up. Just like that, gravity turned the world back on.

"Back where you were."

We un-paused. There's a special kind of whiplash that comes from stopping everything to keep something from becoming news and then immediately resuming your scheduled chaos. It's funny and disorienting and very human. My brain filed it under: If this becomes a bit, it's funny; if it becomes a habit, it's jail.

The car-fire break did something to the team. Humor is glue when it's earned. The next run was cleaner, like we'd collectively unclenched. We moved faster but not sloppy. You could feel that organism thing happen—one body, many parts. No one said "synchronize," but we did. No one said "flow," but it showed up, cool as a new scar.

Afternoon heat stacked itself at a forty-five-degree angle and pressed. We hit a three-structure sequence with a mock market in the middle: tables, tarps, line-of-sight problems everywhere. Role-players argued in two languages and three attitudes. The breacher's ram did its devastating little waltz. The door that never opens, opened. The door that always open reminded us it has agency. We saw the best version of a bad situation—speed meeting caution in a hallway that didn't want guests.

We ate when someone shoved food into our hands. It tasted like the wrapper. Water bottles emptied like they were trying to win a race. Someone invented a sandwich out of beef jerky, a tortilla, and hope. I took a bite and realized my jaw had fallen asleep.

By late afternoon, the village looked like a board game after toddlers—pieces everywhere, rules unclear, everyone confident anyway. We cleaned up, re-rigged, checked batteries like rabbits check for hawks. I swapped socks like a man with ambitions. Jarrod taped a hotspot he named something unprintable. The breacher's ram leaned against a wall like an exhausted rhino.

Dusk came in on a slant. Shadows got longer and smarter. Lights stayed off because lights are tattletales. Someone cracked a Chemlight and tucked it under a cap bill where it made a little alien smile. We got our night orders the way you get bad news from a doctor who's also your friend—kindly, quickly, with eye contact.

Hostage scenario. Limited comms. Multiple entries. Smoke. The part where they test your ability to separate signal from screaming.

I hate hostage scenarios. I love what they do for the brain; I hate what they do to the gut. The math gets mean. The role-player who wants you to fail is good at their job and your heart gets loud. The moral clarity you thought you owned shows up late and out of breath.

We staged on the east side as the last pink scraped off the sky. I could taste the powder ghosts from the day. We stacked. I took my spot, felt the guy behind me breathe, felt the guy in front of me be very, very still. Smoke drifted like a shy cat. Somewhere a door thumped and my body cataloged it: wooden, old hinges, someone impatient.

We went.

Night inside steel is the kind of dark that has texture. Your white-light discipline becomes your personality. My tape-baffled beam found corners like it was writing something down. We cleared one room, then another, the kind that look innocent until they're not. A role-player yelled something I won't repeat and threw an object we were supposed to ignore but absolutely did not, because the limbic system is a prankster.

The hostage was where hostages always are, inconveniently placed, hysterical, and wearing a face that would make a saint fail a test. We practiced all the things we'd been practicing for months- words first, then movement, then hands, then the slow miracle of a situation choosing not to get worse. We didn't get it perfect. I forgot a line I wanted to use and used the right one anyway because it was shorter and kinder. Somebody behind me kept the hall from exploding by being boring on purpose. I love boring. Boring saves lives.

Halfway through the second floor a radio died in the worst way—on, loud, and transmitting a pocket worth of garbage. We fixed it without yelling, which is a sentence I couldn't have written a year ago. You learn to adjust without performing frustration for the room. You learn your breath can be other people's problem or their solution. I'm not saying we were poetry. I am saying the rhymes started hitting.

There was a moment in a stairwell where we could have fallen apart. Smoke had turned the world into wet paper. Someone in the stack coughed a cough with decision-making stuff in it. The guy at the front hesitated for exactly one beat too long and then did the right thing anyway. That's the muscle I came here to grow—the one that moves when your brain is tired and the plan still needs executing.

We hit the objective room with enough control to call it tidy. Role-players did their best Oscar work. We managed not to shoot anyone we loved. We managed to not forget the parts that get forgotten. We exfilled in a way that didn't look like a mistake filmed from three angles. It felt like... gratitude. Not triumph. Gratitude. The team thing had finally clicked at 2:07 a.m., when all of us were at our worst and therefore capable of our best.

Debrief was a heat lamp for the truth. We stood in a smashed circle, sweat coming from places I didn't know were in play, and told each other what we did and why we did it. The instructors' notes were surgical and kind in the mean way kindness is when it wants you to be better. "Your pause at the threshold saved you." "Your pause in the hallway almost killed someone." "You gave away your position with your mouth." "You recovered with your feet." The compliments were rare and therefore nourishing. The critiques were everywhere and free. That's the economy here.

I kept thinking of the car fire and the full-stop silence that fell over fifty people like snow. The way we all went to a knee in unison. The way it came back on with one word. That's what the night felt like, just slower, hundreds of small stops and starts, a shared pulse, a village trying to teach us something without using language.

Day two was the same game with different cards. Less sleep. More dust. The sun came in hot and uninvited. Vehicle ops bled into assaults bled into holds bled into radio checks and the kind of quiet where you can hear your heart deciding if it likes you. We moved as one animal more often than we didn't. When we didn't, we made it shorter and softer. When someone tripped, a hand dragged them back into the stack without judgment, just gravity. I trusted people I couldn't have described to a sketch artist. I put my life behind a voice and it held.

There was a run near sundown that felt like the movie inside my head on the day we signed up for this foolishness. Vehicles rolled. Smoke curled. We bounded across open ground like we weren't born in offices. The breacher's ram went forward with that noble misery and the door surrendered in a way that made everyone feel momentarily taller. Inside, the rooms behaved. The hostage decided not to break the story. We did the work, we didn't freak out, and when we came back into the light, I looked around and thought, "Okay. We earned something today."

Exfil was a dull blur the way good exhaustion always is. Boots off. Sand you didn't put on your body that nevertheless claimed squatters' rights. Water that tasted like apology. The instructors did the final readout with the dignity of people who have done real versions of this and have chosen to treat yours like it matters. They gave us our ledger: where we shined, where we bled, where we got lucky. They didn't say "good job." They said, "Keep showing up." It meant more.

Driving home after SpecOps, I didn't have the same voice in my head I had after earlier weekends. The old voice said, "You didn't die." The new voice said, "We finally moved." It wasn't about me anymore. It hadn't been for a while, but this weekend made it plain. Every drill in the village had been teaching us the grammar for this sentence. The car fire taught us that reality doesn't care about your plan. The breath you hold is either panic or patience, and they look the same until the next command. The night taught us that attention is a weapon you can hand your friends without giving anything away.

At home, I did the usual ritual—the shower that turns brown for the first minute, the gear laid out like casualties in the garage, the boots with a story to tell and no one to impress. I caught myself checking windows with the kind of casual glance that doesn't announce itself. I wrote three lines in a notebook:

- Calm is the only contagious we want.

- Humor is ballast when it's honest.

- Teams are built at 2 a.m., not at noon.

I slept like a man who had been awake for three days and dreamed of nothing. In the morning the house did its thing—backpacks, cereal, the endless, hilarious negotiations of fatherhood. Everything Everywhere All at Once has been my life long before this weekend. The difference now is that the noise doesn't feel like an enemy. It feels like a landscape. You navigate it by breathing.

We haven't made it to Mog Mile yet. That's coming—the long run, the smoke, the chaos that eats maps for breakfast. But this was the turn. This was the weekend where we stopped being guys with gear and started being a team that could be trusted with a problem. The village didn't clap. The desert didn't care. We did. That's enough.

When people ask what SpecOps was like, I usually say: "It's everything you've learned, happening at the same time, with a stopwatch and consequences." If they ask what I learned, I say: "We finally heard each other." Which is corny and also true. I didn't walk away feeling like a hero. I walked away feeling like a hinge—small, necessary, creaky, getting better with use.

Later, when the plateau came and we had to decide whether we wanted different teachers and harder lessons, this weekend was the evidence file I opened. Not because it was perfect. Because it was ours. Because, for a few hard hours in a hot place, we moved like one thing and made the right kind of quiet inside the noise.

And because—if I'm being honest—there's something healthy about a group of grown men, in full kit, in the middle of the desert, taking a synchronized knee while a stranger kicks dirt onto a burning car and you mutter, "Let it burn—adds realism," and everyone pretends not to laugh.

We became a team right then. The night just confirmed it.

THE MILE THAT TRIED TO KILL US

The morning after the long Sunday felt like the world had been put on pause and no one told our bodies. Three hours of sleep in the dirt doesn't restore anything. It just reminds you that exhaustion has layers. You don't recover—you adapt. The instructors didn't need to motivate us. The sun did that on its own. It rose mean, bright, and loud.

We lined up in front of the tower that had been our north star all weekend—the three-story stack of shipping containers that looked like something pulled straight from Iraq. Paint peeling, steel sweating heat. The ground shimmered. The instructors stood in front of us, unreadable, arms crossed. No notes, no lecture. Just two words.

"Mogadishu Mile."

The tone said everything. There would be no handholding. This was the summit push.

They called it that because of what it was meant to be: a tribute to the chaos of the Battle of Mogadishu, when soldiers sprinted through a city under fire, exhausted, carrying their brothers. Our version wasn't life or death. But it was as close as you can come without headlines.

The rules were simple: full kit, full sprint, full contact. We'd move as squads through the entire combat town. Role players would engage with UTMs, airsoft, and blanks. Vehicles would move through alleys. The Bearcat would rumble. The Jeep would scream. Pyro, smoke, shouting. The whole world turned up to eleven.

You weren't expected to win. You were expected to endure.

The whistle blew and everything broke loose.

The first stretch was dust and noise. We pushed through the outer alleyways, stacked up, and cleared corners while instructors screamed positions over radios that crackled like campfires. Every few seconds someone yelled "CONTACT!" and rounds snapped by with the hard plastic sting of simunitions. You felt every hit—your ribs learning Morse code one welt at a time.

We moved in bounding patterns, one squad covering while another advanced. It was textbook in theory, chaos in practice. Comms were half words and half prayer. "Blue two moving!" "Copy—covering right!" "Wait—who's hit?" The Bearcat rolled ahead, its engine howling, kicking up sand. The Jeep followed like a loyal but angry dog, UTMs thumping from its mounted rifle. Smoke grenades turned everything into a fever dream.

The tower disappeared behind us in the haze. We were running blind.

About twenty minutes in, the heat went from background noise to the main event. Sweat soaked everything. The gear added twenty pounds that felt like fifty. I was breathing through a straw. The sun hit the metal buildings and threw back light so harsh it hurt to blink. Somewhere in the chaos, someone laughed—half madness, half relief. It was contagious. You laugh because you're still alive.

We hit our second objective, a row of shipping containers stacked into a makeshift street. Role players were inside, firing blanks from windows, shouting, taunting, making it feel real. One of them tossed a smoke that rolled under a car parked at the base of the rappelling tower. I saw it bounce, hiss, and then flare.

At first, it was just a little orange light. Then it turned into a flame.

"Fire! Fire! Fire!" someone yelled.

The instructors called, "BLACK, BLACK, BLACK!"—the code for full stop. Fifty of us froze mid-step. One of the role players sprinted to the burning car, kicking dirt on it, hands slapping at the flames. For a moment it felt like the whole town held its breath.

111

Then the wind shifted. Smoke and heat hit our faces like a wave. It wasn't simulation anymore. It was real.

He got it out. Barely. The car sat there smoking, half melted, half alive. Someone muttered, "Realism." I whispered, "Let it burn." The instructor shot me a look. Even he cracked a grin.

Then the whistle blew again, and we were back in it.

Something shifted after that. The joking stopped. The adrenaline found a new gear. The Mog Mile had officially become what it was designed to be—a marathon through chaos. The instructors stopped being instructors. They became ghosts on the periphery, watching to see who would keep moving when the plan collapsed.

Every few minutes we'd take contact. UTMs pinged off walls. A role player screamed. Someone's mag dropped and vanished in the dust. You didn't have time to think about tactics anymore. You just reacted. You trusted your team. You kept your muzzle downrange and your feet moving.

That's when I realized this wasn't about skill anymore. It was about staying in motion when motion hurt.

Jarrod took point on the third leg. His voice came through the radio—steady, clipped, surgical. "Move left. Tower's our guide. We're pushing north." He sounded like a man reading from a manual written inside his own head. He was tired but not done. None of us were.

We hit a corner and stacked up behind a cinderblock wall. My hands were shaking from adrenaline and dehydration. My rifle felt twice its weight. I could smell the cordite and plastic from the burned car mixed with the metallic taste of my own breath.

The instructor nearest us yelled, "Next contacts live! Move!"

We did.

112

Rounds started flying again. Someone went down—simulated casualty. We dragged him back by his plate carrier, yelling "Man down!" over the radio. Jarrod and I dropped into cover behind a half wall, returned fire with UTM until the role player called "HIT!" and dropped theatrically.

That's when it hit me: I wasn't scared. Not anymore. I was beyond fear. It was something purer—a weird, calm awareness. Everything slowed. Every movement had purpose. My mind stopped asking questions. It just acted.

That's the boom moment. The point where exhaustion and clarity shake hands.

The final stretch was the real "mile." We regrouped, drenched, half-limping, half-running. The instructors lined the edge of the compound, arms crossed, watching. The Bearcat idled, engine growling like a heartbeat. The Jeep idled behind it. The radio crackled once: "Final leg—full send."

We took off.

It wasn't a sprint. It was a crawl through fire disguised as running. Full kit. Helmet. Rifle. Every step was a negotiation. The sun was brutal, the air thick with smoke. I could taste metal and dust. Every breath came with a sound. I lost count of how many times I thought I'd stop. Every time I did, someone next to me pushed, Jarrod, a firefighter named Dan, a cop from Texas. They kept me moving.

We turned the last corner and saw the tower through the haze. It looked like a cathedral. Three stories of rusted faith. My vision tunneled. My body didn't belong to me anymore. It belonged to the team.

Someone yelled, "Last hundred!" and it sounded like a joke from God.

We ran. Or stumbled. Or whatever word fits for men who are running on fumes and pride. The instructors fired blanks overhead to simulate cover. The sound was biblical. When we crossed the final threshold, the Bearcat lights flashed and the whistle screamed once, long and final.

And then there was silence.

The dust hung in the air like it didn't want to leave. Nobody talked. We were all staring at each other, waiting for someone to break the spell. One of the instructors walked through the group, nodding once at each of us. No speech. No ceremony. Just a nod. Like he was saying, "You made it. You're changed. You'll figure out what that means later."

We dropped gear, found shade, drank water that felt like medicine. My hands were shaking too bad to unscrew the cap. Jarrod took it from me, opened it, handed it back, and said nothing. That's friendship—no need to explain the language of survival.

Someone joked, "I'm not sure if I passed or just didn't die." The instructor smiled. "Same thing."

BACK HOME DEBRIEF

Mogadishu Mile wasn't a test of skill. It was a test of surrender—to exhaustion, to teamwork, to the realization that limits are real but temporary. You find out who you are when there's nothing left to hide behind—no technique, no checklist, no instructor to bail you out. Just you, your breath, and the next step.

When I got home that night, I left my kit on the floor and sat in the shower until the water ran cold. The bruises started to bloom, but my mind was quiet. There's a strange peace in being completely emptied out.

That weekend didn't make me a warrior. It made me honest. It showed me that being "hard to kill" isn't about toughness—it's about resilience, awareness, and the ability to keep moving when the world catches fire around you.

And that's what happened in that desert.

We ran through smoke. We carried each other. We found the
edge of the map.

And for one long, burning mile, we didn't stop.

TOO COMFORTABLE TO BE DANGEROUS

We called it the ceremonial debrief. Which is a fancy way of saying: the first Coors Light after forty-eight hours of simulated violence, dehydration, and tactical poor life choices.

No showers. No clean clothes. Just a layer of Arizona dust thick enough to count as ballistic protection. We stumbled into our usual dive bar five miles from the range—the one with the broken neon beer sign and jukebox that only plays songs about bad decisions.

The bartender saw us, shook her head, and said, "Long weekend?"

"Something like that," I answered.

She slid four Coors Lights down the bar like she was triaging us.

That first sip felt like medicine. Cold enough to sting my lip where a sim round had split it.

Nobody talked at first. Just the clink of cans and the distant hum of the cooler behind the bar. Our bodies were wrecked, but our minds were still replaying the chaos—door breaches, smoke, yelling, the smell of powder in our teeth.

Then Jarrod leaned back and said the line that broke us all open.

"Dude... what the *fuck* just happened?"

We lost it.

Full-on laughter. Bent-over, teary-eyed, gasping-for-air laughter.

The kind that comes after you survive something that could've gone worse in at least eight different ways.

"Remember when you threw that smoke grenade into the wind?"

"I was testing wind drift!"

"You were testing the limits of insurance coverage."

"Science has risks."

Someone mentioned the role-player who got too into his part and tried to stab me with a plastic knife. Another brought up my now-famous tripping incident with the breaching ram.

"Hey," I said, "gravity's undefeated."

We laughed until we hurt. The waitress dropped fries and didn't even flinch when one of us said something about simulated casualties. She'd seen this before—guys who train too hard and talk too loud.

For a while, the noise, the light, the salt of the fries—it all felt like oxygen.

Then the instructors walked in.

Same crew. Same table. Same whiskey order.

They looked like stone statues that could shoot.

We raised our beers in respect. They nodded back.

Then they started talking—war stories, training stories, the same ones we'd already memorized.

Halfway through the first story, I realized I could predict the next five sentences.

Every laugh, every beat, every moral.

And that's when it hit me:

We're not the new guys anymore. We're the rerun.

At first, it felt wrong to even think that.

These were the men who had taken us from clueless civilians to semi-capable humans who could breach a door without dying. They'd forged us.

But that's what happens when you stay in one forge too long—you start to take its shape.

Same range.

Same drills.

Same jokes about the guy who negligent discharged into the dirt berm.

Same everything.

The worst part?

We were good now.

And good is the last stop before comfortable.

The next weekend proved it.

We showed up out of habit, not hunger.

Same sunrise, same gravel crunch under boots, same faint smell of sunscreen and CLP.

We stacked up. Breached. Cleared. Moved. Reloaded.

Everything perfect. Too perfect.

No adrenaline spikes. No panic.

Just repetition with nice form.

It was like tactical karaoke—you knew every word, but the song had lost its soul.

During a break, I caught myself teaching a new guy how to pie a corner—using the instructor's exact phrasing.

That's when I knew I wasn't training anymore.

I was performing.

That night, after the gear was packed, Jarrod and I sat in the truck with the windows down, dust swirling in the headlights.

"You ever feel like we're looping?" he asked.

"Like Groundhog Day?"

"Exactly. But with more bruises and less Bill Murray."

We laughed, but quietly.

Then he said it:

"I think we're done here."

He didn't mean quitting. He meant graduating.

And he was right.

Leaving felt like betrayal.

Marauders wasn't just a range—it was our forge.

Our friends. Our teachers. Our tribe.

But even tribes can turn into cages.

Same voices. Same gospel. Same rhythm of "move, shoot, communicate."

We needed friction again.

I didn't want to quit. I wanted to struggle again.

Because that's where growth lives—on the edge of "I don't know if I can do this."

And I missed that edge.

A few days later I was in the garage cleaning my rifle. CLP in the air, soft country on the radio, hands moving on muscle memory.

Every scuff on that gun told a story.

The tower rappel.

The first *ping* off steel.

The moment I learned fear and focus are the same feeling until you breathe.

Marauders had given me everything: skill, confidence, brothership.

But the fuse had burned down.

That's not failure—it's proof you finished the circuit.

The next Saturday, Jarrod showed up at my house with his laptop and a case of beer.

He dropped it on the table and said, "We need something new."

We scrolled through websites for hours—logos with skulls, Latin mottos, and the word *OPERATOR* in bold font.

"Too mall ninja," I said.

"Too militia."

"Too cult like."

"Too far."

Then he stopped scrolling.

"Executive Protection," he said. "Civilian-accessible. Real clients. Real-world detail work."

He turned the screen toward me.

The picture was a man in plain clothes scanning a crowd. Calm. Unnoticed. Alone.

It looked nothing like the desert chaos we were used to.

And that was the point.

"Different?" he asked.

"Different," I said.

We read the course description. Driving, awareness, threat assessment.

The instructor: Fred.

No beard photos, no military flexing. Just bullet points and credibility.

"This guy's legit," Jarrod said.

"Yeah," I said. "But I don't think I can swing another weekend off right now."

He looked at me. "You go. Bring it back."

121

And that was that.

For the first time, it wasn't *we*, it was *me*.

The week before the course, I stripped my kit down to the essentials—no extra pouches, no vanity gear. Just what mattered.

Funny thing about cleaning gear: it always ends up cleaning your head, too.

I realized I'd built comfort into my loadout.

The extra gear was just armor for my ego.

I packed light.

For once, I wanted to show up feeling like the rookie again.

The morning of the course, I drove across town alone.

No banter. No playlist. No Jarrod adjusting the GPS from the passenger seat.

The cab was quiet except for my heartbeat.

I realized I hadn't done a class solo since the beginning.

It felt right—and terrifying.

The GPS led me to a neighborhood so normal it felt fake.

Perfect lawns. Flag on every porch. Minivan in every driveway.

I double-checked the address.

"This can't be it," I muttered.

But it was.

I sat there for a minute, watching sprinklers turn and light shift across the street. The kind of stillness that makes you second-guess yourself.

Finally, I shut off the engine.

"Alright," I said to no one. "Let's see what happens."

Walking up that path felt heavier than any ruck I'd carried. Not physically—mentally. Every step away from the truck was a step out of the comfort I'd built.

Before I could knock, the door opened.

A man in a clean button-up stepped out.

No belt gear. No bravado.

Just presence.

"Fred," I said, offering my hand.

He looked at it, then at me.

"You ready to learn how this works in the real world?"

"Yeah," I said. "I think I am."

He nodded once. Then walked right past me, straight to my truck, opened the door, and said, "I'm driving."

I stood there for a beat, processing the reversal.

Boom moment.

For the first time since this whole thing began, I wasn't part of a team.

I was the detail.

I was the student.

And the world just got a lot bigger.

BACK HOME DEBRIEF

You never forget your first forge. Marauders was ours.

It took two suburban dads and made them capable.
Confident. Hungry.

But the forge can't be forever. Stay too long, and the fire stops
shaping you—it just burns.

This time, the road split.

Jarrod stayed with the tribe.

I went solo.

Not out of ego—out of necessity.

Because in every protector's journey, there's a point where
you have to walk alone.

No one watching. No one catching your mistakes.

Just you, your decisions, and the silence between them.

That's where growth hides.

And it's where I found it.

Marauders gave me the *bang*.

But this—this was the beginning of the *boom*.

I packed up my gear, cracked a beer, and wrote one line in my notebook before heading to bed:

Protection isn't a team sport when it counts.

I didn't know it yet, but that was foreshadowing for everything that came next.

Haley D7. The moments where you face yourself and there's nowhere left to hide.

Some lessons you can only learn with a buddy.

And some you have to face alone.

This was the start of that second kind.

THE DAY I LEARNED HOW TO SEE

You can only run a drill so many times before you start to hear the echo. Same doors. Same dust. Same jokes I could lip-sync. The day I realized I could predict an instructor's critique like a sitcom punchline, something quiet in me shut off. I didn't want louder. I wanted truer. I wanted real rooms with real people and consequences that didn't wait for a whistle.

Marauders had given me a taste of it—planning, movement, that first sip of executive-protection logic—but it was still weekend lightning in a bottle. I needed the storm that lives over an actual city. And I needed to go alone. No Jarrod in the passenger seat. No shared playlist or last-minute sarcasm to bleed off nerves. Just me and whatever this next door opened onto.

Enter Fred.

I found him the way civilians find a lot of trouble: Instagram. His page was clean—no mall-ninja cosplay, no ego monologues. People I respected followed him. The bio was an understatement that turned out to be a résumé: seasoned professional; career executive-protection professional; author for more magazines than I knew existed; the kind of teacher other teachers quote. Guys whispered that his private firearms collection made museums jealous—rare pieces with stories that sound impossible until he quietly produces provenance.

I signed up for a pistol class and showed up early, because when you go alone you either arrive early or you arrive scared. Fred moved through the line like calm with elbows. Shirt tucked, eyes soft, presence that made a room sit up without realizing it was doing push-ups. He corrected grips like a watchmaker, fixed my stance with two fingers and an economy of words: "There. Now let the gun speak in complete sentences."

We shot. We learned. We laughed exactly once every twenty minutes because he understood that humor, like caffeine, works best in measured doses. He filmed a little, took notes no one saw, and never raised his voice. At the end, he shook my hand and said, "You did the work. Come back if you want to do the job."

Two months later, I was in a Walmart on a Tuesday buying batteries and snacks for the boys when a face I recognized stared at me from the magazine rack. Mine. I blinked. Picked it up. There I was—front cover—mid-string, posture corrected, language of his class written across my body like I'd rehearsed it for years. Inside, a full feature on training—written by Fred.

"Holy—" I didn't finish the sentence. I bought two copies like a suspicious relative and stood in the parking lot under a sky that suddenly looked like it knew my name. It wasn't fame; it was permission. I was a civilian who had been invited, however briefly, into print by a professional whose words shaped this world. It felt like the map just added a road I didn't know I was allowed to drive.

That's how I ended up signing up for his three-day executive-protection course. Solo. Just my own voice and a note in the calendar that read: do not flinch.

We started in a place built for distractions—the Tilted Kilt. Neutral ground. Plenty of parking. Terrible acoustics for secrets. The choice was instructional before class began: if you can make good decisions in a room designed to make you stupid, you'll do fine in public. Fred arrived without announcement; the air just recalibrated around him. Button-down. Watch that had earned its scratches. He unfolded a map like a priest unveiling the relic that matters.

"You're the detail," he said. "I'm the principal. Two errands. Lunch. A public stop you won't have time to rehearse. Most of this is early decisions, not heroic ones."

We assigned roles and drew routes that looked competent until he erased one domino from the middle and asked a gentle question that collapsed the chain. He let the room teach the rest: the big window that made us silhouettes, the door swing that traps you on the wrong hinge, the way noise arranges people into patterns if you stop pretending it won't. He didn't tell us to be invisible. He told us to be uninteresting.

Next morning, I pulled up to his house alone. No banter in the cab. No witness to my nerves. He opened the door like we were mid-sentence, walked past me to the truck, and said, "Keys." He adjusted the mirror a quarter inch, the seat two clicks, and scanned the interior without making it a performance. "We're hot."

Boom moment. Not loud. The mission had started and nobody cued the music.

I wish I could tell you I arrived in peak form. The truth is I was recovering from a stomach flu that had made war on my insides the day before, and the first block involved mild combatives. We were in a corporate studio—the Center Mass podcast office space—learning to move people without breaking them when Fred said, almost conversationally, "If he won't go, there's a way to convince the gut to speak with the brain." He demonstrated a knuckle-roll body shot at quarter power. My soul tried to exit through the roof. Every muscle below the belt clenched like it had a meeting with the Board of Directors.

I thought, very distinctly: do not become a cautionary tale on Day One.

I didn't. I breathed. I learned to steer with my feet and my voice. And when the room laughed at the right time, my pride didn't need to.

The course was a study in restraint. Route planning, arrival and departure choreography, seating, timing, and the humility to pick a different restaurant because the parking lot tells you more about a place than the menu ever will. We drilled purse-snatches, attention breaks, and the subtle physics of moving a human who doesn't know they're in your way. He taught pace like it was a language—too fast and you drag the principal, too slow and the crowd becomes a net.

Lunch was its own lesson. He chose a table with his back to a wall and our exfil written into the walkway. He didn't say, "Don't face the door." He just sat where seeing wasn't a job; it was an option. His hands lived where they could work without declaring themselves the main characters. I copied without making it a mime act.

The public stop was a Japanese cultural festival downtown. Drums. Flags. Food trucks. A thousand beautiful distractions. He told us the only thing that matters in crowds: leave early. We walked a loose triangle—close, outside, and long eyes. We noticed generators and cords and toddler flight paths and the quiet gravity of people who orbit a group photo without belonging to it. We didn't hunt bad guys. We hunted timing. It turns out timing is what bad guys rent when they want to look like chance.

Ten minutes before my ego wanted to, we turned our feet toward the exit. That single act prevented a hundred small negotiations from becoming one large problem. Outside, I finally exhaled like I hadn't been doing it right for an hour.

Between reps, Fred told stories the way good mentors do—once, briefly, with the lesson hidden inside. A client who survived because the team respected a boring hunch. A route that died on paper because a parade nobody cared about last year had decided to matter. He never bragged; he cited. Once, in a lull, someone asked about a rifle none of us had ever handled. He smiled the kind of smile you wear when you know where history sleeps and said, "Some pieces live in quiet rooms. We visit, we learn, we put them back." Then we went back to work.

His debriefs were surgical and kind in the way honesty is when it wants you to keep showing up. He told me six things I didn't see and one thing I did perfectly. The perfect thing was small—turning my feet before I signaled the move at the demo so the crowd read my intention a half-second early. The misses were smaller: I drifted too fast once and made the

129

principal obey me; I walked through the wrong side of a door swing and invited an unnecessary touch; I let my face publish what my eyes had noticed. "Keep the eyes honest," he said. "Leave the face out of the press release."

By the end of Day Three I had stopped trying to look professional and started trying to be useful. EP wasn't about swagger. It was logistics and love. It was choosing the parking spot your future self will thank you for. It was letting the loudest part of you be the plan, not the posture.

A week later, Fred had me on the Skillset podcast to talk through civilian takeaways. I kept waiting for someone to tap me on the shoulder and ask if I was lost. No one did. I wasn't a peer, exactly. But I wasn't a tourist anymore either. I was a man who had learned to leave early.

Back home, everything nudged a degree toward deliberate. I started booking hotel floors between three and six because physics loves ladders. I walked the stairwell once when I wasn't tired so I could walk it twice when I was. I picked restaurant tables where the kids could spill fries and I could still see the door without pretending it's a personality trait. I took stickers off the back window—no one needs to know where my kids go to school, what I shoot, or who I voted for. My car stopped writing my biography for strangers bored enough to read it.

I checked timing instead of checking boxes. What time the grocery store turns from families into men walking too slowly with two things in a basket. What time the gas station becomes a survey of bad decisions. What time the school drop-off line teaches you what pattern of impatience equals a fender-bender. EP bled into fatherhood without needing a press release.

Marauders had given me the urge to move. Fred gave me the discipline to wait. Marauders taught me to enter a room with conviction. Fred taught me to choose the right room in the first place. If I ever teach, I'll do it like he does—patient, precise, a text away when your students hit a wall.

The magazine cover went in a frame that lives in my office. Not because I think I'm important. Because it reminds me that a professional I respect saw a civilian trying, and decided to say, in print, "Keep going."

So I did.

BACK HOME DEBRIEF

Before Fred, I thought preparedness was a growl. After Fred, I know it's a calendar. It's ten minutes early so the route is yours. It's reading rooms like weather—patterns first, storms later. It's picking a seat where seeing is easy and leaving is easier. It's the smallest signal removed from your car and the smallest argument you never had because you stepped away when your gut whispered not today.

Executive protection didn't turn me into a bodyguard. It turned me into a boring man in the right places. Boring is how you become hard to corner, hard to surprise, and easy to love when your family just wants a dad who gets them home. I still train loud when it's time for loud, but most days the work is quiet: one-inch adjustments, early decisions. Logistics as love.

That's the cover story—literally and otherwise. A magazine on a rack in a fluorescent aisle told me I wasn't just playing dress-up anymore. A medic-turned-professional gave me the tools to protect what matters without turning my life into a performance. The rest of the book is me proving I heard him.

THE WORK THAT FINDS YOU

I didn't join The Fund because I was the right man for the job.

Or because I was noble.

Or because I had some deep understanding of service, trauma, or the first responder world.

I joined because Jarrod texted me a link at 10:42 p.m. — a job posting wedged between a breaching meme and whatever the algorithm was hallucinating that week — and those four fateful words:

"You should do this."

It was a part-time marketing role for a nonprofit I'd never heard of. No flashy graphics. No big pitch. Just:

"Support training access for first responders."

That was it.

I didn't know about the national training deficit.

I didn't know departments were sending people into danger with skills held together by duct tape and luck.

I didn't know that the thing I was clicking on would become the emotional backbone of my adult life.

All I knew was that "marketing" was something I could do.

Nothing heroic.

Nothing transformative.

Just something helpful.

And at that moment in my life, being useful felt like oxygen.

So I applied.

Not because I was ready.

Because I wanted to matter.

I had no idea how much this decision was about to matter back.

THE INTERVIEW

Brandy appeared on my screen like someone who had already handled everything I was about to struggle with.

No dramatics.

No chest-thumping.

No "I run a nonprofit" performance.

Just calm capability in human form.

"Tell me why you applied," she said.

I started talking — about training weekends at Marauders, about learning under instructors who'd seen real violence, about the gap between what officers need and what budgets allow. I told her the mission made sense to me, even though I couldn't yet articulate why.

She listened.

Really listened.

Then she said something casually that hit like a thrown wrench:

"Well, just so you're aware... Tim helps out here."

I blinked. Once. Twice.

"...Tim who?"

She raised an eyebrow as if clarifying gravity.

"Tim Kennedy."

For anyone outside this world:

Tim Kennedy is a Special Forces Green Beret, sniper, UFC fighter, counterterrorism guy, and full-time chaos deity. The sort of man whose handshake feels like it lifts your credit score. He is famous for coining the phrase be "hard to kill".

And I was applying for a marketing role in his vicinity?

Brandy must've read the panic on my face because she laughed.

"He's not heavily involved. He helps where he can. Don't rely on him."

I nodded — the kind of nod that says, I am absolutely going to rely on him just by being aware he exists.

She offered me the role on the spot.

And that should've been the big moment.

But it wasn't.

Not even close.

NIGHTS AND WEEKENDS

The Fund wasn't an organization.

It was a constellation of tired people doing their best in the margins of their already chaotic lives.

Volunteers in different states.

No office.

No payroll.

No systems.

No SOPs.

No org chart.

Just heart.

People squeezing service into:

- the ten minutes before a kid woke up,

- the fifteen minutes after dinner,

- the two hours after everyone else went to sleep.

I did the marketing — the raffles, the patch drops, the campaigns, the emails, the scramble-to-fix-the-website-at-midnight emergencies.

It was messy.

But it felt alive.

Then came the call that changed everything.

THE OFFICER

It was one of those "step outside your office so your coworkers don't overhear" calls.

I answered casually:

"Hey, this is Erik."

There was wind on the line.

A long inhale.

A pause that felt heavier than it should.

He told me he was a police officer.

He wanted to volunteer for the Fund.

He liked our mission.

Then his voice broke — in that human, unchosen way.

He told me he'd been involved in a shooting.

He told me the suspect was a kid.

I didn't speak.

Because what do you say to that?

He kept talking because he needed to.

Then he said the sentence that pinned itself to my chest:

"If I'd had this training... maybe that wouldn't have happened."

Not guilt.

Not blame.

Not justification.

Truth.

Raw.

Quiet.

Unavoidable.

That moment rearranged me.

The world tilted.

The asphalt under my feet felt different.

The noise of cars passing became background to the weight of what he'd just shared.

This wasn't theory.

This wasn't a volunteer gig.

This wasn't a hobby.

This was life and death, whispered to me on a phone call behind a strip-mall office.

The Fund became personal in an instant.

I just didn't know how personal it was about to become.

BRANDY

Brandy wasn't the public face or the loud cheerleader.

She was the infrastructure.

The invisible machinery.

The glue.

She knew every volunteer, every donor, every department, every officer.

She carried The Fund in her head.

Quietly.

Competently.

Without ego.

She didn't chase credit.

She chased outcomes.

Then one morning, she was gone.

A brain aneurysm.

No warning.

No goodbye.

One day she was answering emails, coordinating scholarships, solving problems.

The next day the group chat was silent.

The Fund didn't have continuity plans.

It didn't have redundancies.

It didn't have someone else who knew the systems.

It had Brandy.

And then it didn't.

I didn't know what to do.

I didn't know what to say.

I didn't know how to carry a mission that she had held with such grace.

Then the board called.

"Erik... we want you to take over.

We want you to be the Managing Director."

And everything inside me said:

Absolutely not.

I'm not qualified.

I'm not ready.

I'm not the person she was.

But grief has a way of making the next step obvious, even if it's terrifying.

 Brandy's last message to me — the last line she ever sent — was:

"Whatever you do, just keep showing up."

So I did.

Reluctantly.

Confused.

Unequipped.

Sweaty.

But I showed up.

STEPPING INTO THE FIRE

Saying yes to becoming Managing Director, felt like strapping on a plate carrier for the first time:

- too heavy

- too complicated

- pinching places I didn't know could pinch

- and giving everyone around me the dangerous impression that I somehow knew what I was doing

I didn't.

I knew how to market.

I knew how to write.

I knew how to show up.

I did NOT know how to run a nonprofit.

I didn't know the tax laws.

Didn't know the software.

Didn't know the onboarding process.

Didn't know the financial reporting requirements.

Didn't know what I didn't know.

So I did what any responsible adult in over his head does:

I Googled EVERYTHING.

"How to manage a nonprofit."

"What is a 501(c)(3)?"

"What counts as restricted funds?"

"How to organize donor databases without crying?"

"Is excessive sweating deadly?"

No one tells you that leadership isn't competence — it's consent.

You agree to figure it out.

You agree to carry things you didn't ask to carry.

You agree to walk through the mess because someone has to, and that someone might as well be you.

The Fund didn't stop moving.

It didn't wait for me to catch up.

There were scholarship requests.

Departments waiting on answers.

Volunteers waiting on direction.

Invoices.

Emails.

Questions.

The work didn't slow down just because I didn't know what I was doing.

So neither could I.

THE REBUILD BEGINS

If the Fund had a soul, it was Brandy.

If it had a skeleton, it was... chaos.

When she passed, what she left behind wasn't disorganization — it was instinct.

She had run the entire operation by feel.

Her memory was the database.

Her relationships were the infrastructure.

Her compassion was the operating system.

Without her, everything she held together gently fell to the table like someone had cut the strings of a marionette.

There were:

- half-labeled folders

- emails only she understood

- spreadsheets that looked like archeological digs

- donors waiting on updates

- officers waiting on approvals

- volunteers waiting on instruction

- vendors waiting on direction

None of it was her fault.

She had built a mission — not a machine.

Now it was my turn to build the machine that could carry the mission forward.

So I rebuilt everything.

Piece by piece.

Late night after late night.

Break by break.

Step by fragile step.

Scholarship intake systems.

Donor CRM organization.

Outreach cycles.

Volunteer communication frameworks.

Financial tracking that wouldn't give an IRS auditor a stroke.

It wasn't glamorous.

It wasn't Instagram-worthy.

It wasn't the kind of thing you film in slow motion with epic music.

It was work.

The right kind.

The kind that makes you grow whether you want to or not.

THE WEIGHT OF REAL PEOPLE

The more I rebuilt, the more I realized how heavy the mission actually was.

Because every spreadsheet row wasn't a number — it was a person.

A cop who'd been punched in the face by life so many times they'd forgotten what normal looked like.

A medic who'd held someone's last breath.

A firefighter who'd crawled through smoke thick enough to taste.

A dispatcher who'd listened to screams the public never hears.

And they needed training.

Real training.

Life-saving training.

Not to be heroes.

To go home.

Departments didn't have budgets for it.

Unions didn't always have pathways for it.

Systems weren't designed to prioritize it.

The Fund was the bridge.

And suddenly, I was the bridge-builder.

The weight of that wasn't crushing.

It was clarifying.

Every name was a responsibility.

Every request was a life.

Every approval mattered.

Every delay mattered.

It matured me in ways I didn't expect and honestly didn't feel ready for.

This wasn't "doing good."

This was stewardship.

THE UNIVERSE TESTS YOU BEFORE IT PROMOTES YOU

There's a pattern I've noticed in life:

The moment you finally accept responsibility...

The universe immediately sends a test to see if you meant it.

For me, that test came from a Texas area code.

It came with gunfire in the background.

It came with a voice I absolutely did not expect to hear on the other end of my phone.

145

It came in the most absurd, hilarious form possible.

And it arrived exactly when I was starting to doubt whether I belonged in this world at all.

That moment deserves its own stage.

That's Part 3.

But before we get there, there's one more thing you have to understand:

I didn't feel worthy.

I didn't feel ready.

I didn't feel confident.

But I kept showing up.

And showing up, it turns out, is how you move from who you are to who you need to be for the people who are counting on you.

THE CALL FROM TEXAS

I was in the kitchen.

Not doing anything heroic.

Not doing anything important.

I was staring into the pantry like a man hoping snacks would solve organizational problems.

Hannah was in the living room.

The kids were asleep.

The house was finally still — which is the exact moment the universe loves to commit chaos.

My phone buzzed.

Texas number.

For context:

No one from Texas calls me unless one of the following is happening:

1.   I've won a sweepstakes I didn't enter.

2.   A telemarketer is aggressively hopeful.

3.   A divine punishment is underway.

4.   A military-adjacent demigod has misdialed.

I answered anyway.

"Hey, this is Erik."

There was a sound on the line.

Not static.

Not wind.

Not "bad connection."

Gunfire.

Actual gunfire.

Like someone was microwaving bullets.

Before I could process anything, a voice came through:

"Hey man, it's Tim."

Everything in my body failed simultaneously.

My nervous system hit CTRL+ALT+DEL.

My sweat glands filed for emancipation.

My soul left my body and hovered somewhere near the ceiling fan.

Let me be absolutely clear for anyone reading this later:

A Special Forces Green Beret, sniper, UFC fighter, counterterrorism operator, and real-life superhero just cold-called me during target practice.

My internal monologue was NOT noble.

It was:

- Why is he calling me?

- Is this an accident?

- Is this how I die? Via voicemail?

- Is he hunting someone? Am I the someone?

- Should I hide behind the kitchen island?

Meanwhile, out loud, I said — in a voice that cracked like a middle-school trombone—

"Oh... hey buddy!"

Buddy.

I called a Green Beret "buddy."

While he was actively shooting.

He kept talking like this was the most normal call in America.

He welcomed me into the Managing Director role.

He said he appreciated what I was doing.

He gave me contact info and a few insights about what had worked in the past.

I don't remember any of it.

Because I was sweating so hard the phone almost slipped out of my hand and into the dog bowl.

I paced the kitchen like a man preparing to flee his own home.

My voice jumped two octaves.

My eyes kept darting toward the windows as if someone was about to rappel into the backyard.

He was warm.

Direct.

Supportive.

Kind.

And that somehow made it WORSE.

Because now the fear mixed with respect.

Which is a lethal combination for my personality.

He wrapped up the call in under two minutes.

We hung up.

I stood perfectly still for ten seconds, trying to convince my soul to get back into my body.

Then I walked into the living room — drenched, shaking, looking like someone had just shoved me through a car wash on "Maximum Shame" mode.

Hannah looked up from the couch.

She blinked twice.

"Why are you so sweaty?"

I swallowed.

"That... was Tim."

Her eyebrows hit her hairline.

"Excuse me, WHO called you?"

I didn't have the emotional vocabulary to answer that question, so I just stood there, sweating like a hostage.

It was absurd.

Ridiculous.

Hysterical.

But also — and this is the part that sits under your ribs — important.

Because for the first time since Brandy passed, someone in the outside world was saying:

You belong here.

This matters.

Keep going.

It didn't come as a compliment.

Or a pep talk.

Or a "rah-rah" motivational thing.

It came in the form of a Special Forces operator casually calling a suburban dad during target practice.

The universe has a sense of humor.

A dark one.

THE SHIFT AFTER THE CALL

Something in me changed that night.

Not confidence.

Not swagger.

Not some delusional "I'm the guy now" energy.

Just steadiness.

A new internal posture.

Because if someone like Tim — someone who has seen pressure, violence, responsibility, and consequence at the extreme edge — took even 90 seconds to acknowledge what I was doing...

Then maybe I wasn't pretending anymore.

Maybe I was actually carrying something real.

Not perfectly.

Not cleanly.

Not without fear.

But faithfully.

That call wasn't a promotion.

It was a calibration.

A reminder that the work mattered.

That Brandy's legacy mattered.

That the mission was bigger than my doubt.

And that showing up — even when I felt completely out of my depth — was the right path forward.

It was the funniest moment of my life.

And one of the most formative.

A perfect midpoint.

A cinematic hinge.

The moment the chapter turns from grief and confusion toward clarity and purpose.

And now the story deepens.

Because after the laughter fades, the work remains.

And the next section — Part 4 — is the quiet rising arc of that work taking shape.

AFTER THE CALL: THE QUIET TURN

I didn't sleep much that night.

Not because I was anxious.

Not because I was panicked.

Not because my body had attempted to sweat itself into a smaller size.

Because something in me had shifted — a real shift, not the kind Instagram pretends you can have in a Hardo Motivational Carousel™.

Clarity has a sound.

It's quiet.

Not gentle, exactly — but precise.

That call from Tim wasn't about him.

It wasn't about me.

It wasn't about "being chosen."

It was a reminder of the stakes.

A reminder that the mission mattered — enough for people far more capable than me to reach out.

A reminder that:

Responsibility isn't something you volunteer for.

It's something you accept.

And accept.

And accept again.

So the next morning, I put my feet on the floor, stood up, exhaled, and walked into the day with a different posture.

Not taller.

Just more committed.

THE REAL REBUILD BEGINS

The Fund didn't magically reorganize itself because I had an emotional breakthrough.

It still looked like:

- a thousand half-finished tasks

- a digital warehouse of outdated spreadsheets

- role confusion

- donor confusion

- volunteer drift

- and a backlog of officers whose requests were gathering dust

It wasn't chaos because people didn't care.

It was chaos because people did care — they were just human, overworked, and trying to serve with whatever scraps of time they had.

So I rebuilt.

Not as a hero.

Not as a visionary.

Not as someone standing on a moral high ground.

As a guy with a laptop, a mission, and a stack of responsibilities taller than his confidence.

I rebuilt the scholarship intake system so it didn't collapse if someone sneezed too hard.

I rebuilt the donor pipeline so no one felt forgotten.

I rebuilt the volunteer communications so no one drifted into silent burnout.

I rebuilt the financial tracking so it didn't resemble a conspiracy board.

Some nights I stared at the screen so long my eyes felt like hot sand.

Some nights I typed with the emotional energy of a man banging coconuts together.

Some nights I almost asked Hannah, "Is this too much?"

But she already knew the answer.

And so did I.

Because every fix — every small, quiet fix — kept the mission alive.

THE FIRST WINS THAT MATTERED

It didn't happen all at once.

It happened like this:

One night, I sent out three scholarship approvals.

155

The next morning: one thank-you email.

The next week: six new applications.

The next batch: a message from an officer saying:

"You guys kept me in the fight."

Another wrote:

"My confidence is back."

Another:

"I feel like I can breathe again."

Those weren't compliments.

They were confirmation.

Proof that the work Brandy started wasn't fading into the ether.

Proof that the world was still being changed in tiny, invisible ways — exactly the kind she believed in.

And it hit me:

Training isn't about looking tactical.

It's about:

- a medic steadying her hands

- a firefighter reading a room faster

- a cop resisting panic instead of acting from it

- a dispatcher making the right call under pressure

- someone surviving a moment that swallows lesser-prepared people whole

The Fund wasn't charity.

It was capacity.

Capacity meant someone got to go home.

Capacity meant someone didn't freeze.

Capacity meant a mistake wasn't fatal.

These weren't heroic stories.

They were human ones.

And human ones matter the most.

THE WEIGHT OF HER LEGACY

The deeper into the rebuild I got, the more I felt Brandy's presence — not in a mystical way, but in a practical one.

Her fingerprints were on everything.

On workflows she half-built.

On notes she left in margins.

On emails that trailed off mid-thought like she meant to finish them the next day.

On the compassion embedded in every process she created.

She didn't leave a manual.

She left a pattern.

A pattern of service.

A pattern of care.

A pattern of showing up when no one asked and when no one was watching.

Some nights I'd sit alone at the kitchen table, surrounded by empty water bottles and the glow of the laptop, reading through old messages she'd written to volunteers or officers.

They weren't grand or performative.

They were small.

Small and impossibly kind.

Small and impossibly important.

That's when I realized:

I wasn't continuing her work.

I was being shaped by it.

There's a difference.

Continuing a legacy feels like pressure.

Being shaped by a legacy feels like inheritance.

And this chapter — this entire season of my life — became about earning what she left behind.

Not by being her.

By being responsible to the mission she carried.

THE QUIET TRANSFORMATION

Transformation doesn't happen during big moments.

It happens when no one is around.

The first sign I was changing wasn't dramatic.

I noticed I wasn't flinching at the workload anymore.

I wasn't doubting whether I belonged.

I wasn't asking, "Why me?"

I was asking:

"What's next?

What else can I fix?

Who else can we help?"

Responsibility doesn't care about your fear.

It cares about your follow-through.

And for the first time, I wasn't doing the work to avoid failure.

I was doing it because the mission deserved someone steady.

The Fund wasn't a burden anymore.

It was a compass.

A direction.

A reminder that purpose doesn't spark — it burns slow and steady, like coals waiting for breath.

THE FUND GROWS UP

As structure returned, so did momentum.

We built:

- an application pipeline that didn't break under weight

- donor and sponsor systems that made sense

- volunteer workflows that actually worked

- reporting processes that kept us accountable

- simple but solid financial controls

- a communication rhythm that kept everyone looped in

It wasn't glamorous.

It was competent.

And competence is what Brandy deserved.

It's what officers deserved.

It's what the mission deserved.

One night, a volunteer who had known Brandy far longer than I had emailed me.

Just one line:

"You're doing right by her."

I leaned back in my chair and let those words land.

Not as praise.

As permission.

As if somewhere in the messy rebuild, I had stopped trying to fill her space and started holding up my own corner of the mission.

And that was enough.

THE ROAD BEGINS TO OPEN

As things stabilized, invitations started appearing:

- partnership opportunities

- event requests

- introductions

- collaborative offers

- officers spreading the word

- trainers wanting to support

The mission was no longer limping.

It was moving.

Growing.

Connecting.

Reaching people we never would've met otherwise.

Then a volunteer messaged:

"You guys going to SHOT Show this year?"

I didn't laugh this time.

I paused.

Because for the first time, it didn't feel absurd.

The Fund wasn't a tiny volunteer project anymore.

It wasn't a fragile thing held together by grief and goodwill.

It was becoming an organization.

A presence.

A community.

And I was becoming the kind of man who could stand inside that world without apologizing for breathing.

SHOT Show wasn't the next chapter yet.

It was just the horizon.

A signal that the world was about to widen.

A reminder that growth doesn't happen in isolation.

And that if I kept showing up —

through grief, through confusion, through humor, through sweat, through doubt —doors would continue to open.

Not because I deserved them.

But because the mission did.

WHAT SERVICE REALLY LOOKS LIKE

People glamorize service.

They wrap it in flags and fanfare and perfectly lit hero shots.

They post quotes about duty in fancy fonts.

They imagine it's loud, cinematic, and instantly recognizable.

But service — real service — is almost always quiet.

It's staying up late with a laptop that keeps freezing.

It's answering officers' messages at 11:30 p.m. when you're half-asleep.

It's fixing a spreadsheet nobody will ever see.

It's holding space for strangers in ways they may never know about.

It's showing up again, and again, and again...even when no one is clapping, no one is cheering, and no one is watching.

Service is the willingness to carry something that matters even when nobody will ever know you did.

Somewhere deep into the rebuild, I realized something uncomfortable:

I wasn't doing this as a volunteer anymore.

I wasn't doing it to feel involved.

I wasn't doing it for pride, or identity, or meaning.

I was doing it as a steward.

Because if something is worth preserving —

if something is worth fighting for —someone has to be the one who stands up and says:

"I've got it.

I'll hold this."

And that realization reshaped the room inside me.

I stopped trying to measure whether I was good enough.

I stopped asking if I was the right person.

I stopped doubting whether I belonged.

I simply showed up.

And showing up, I've learned, is how responsibility becomes readiness.

BRANDY'S SHADOW, BRANDY'S LIGHT

I carried Brandy with me through all of it.

Not as a ghost, not as a memory I couldn't let go of —but as a presence.

Her patterns were everywhere:

- The way she wrote emails.

- The way she talked to officers.

- The way she treated people with patience.

- The way she made every volunteer feel like part of something.

- The way she led without needing anyone to tell her she was leading.

Her work didn't echo loudly.

It resonated quietly.

The kind of resonance that doesn't fade when a person leaves —it expands.

One night, I found an old message thread she'd left behind.

Simple notes.

A follow-up reminder.

A task she meant to finish.

A gentle instruction to check in with someone going through a difficult time.

The last line stopped me:

"Whatever you do, just keep showing up."

It wasn't intended as a final lesson.

It wasn't a slogan or a life philosophy.

It was a practical note for an ordinary day.

But after she passed, it became a mandate.

A compass.

A promise I didn't fully understand when she sent it —

but one I was slowly growing into.

Showing up wasn't just the work.

165

It was the legacy.

THE QUIET WINS

Transformation doesn't arrive with trumpets.

It arrives through repetition.

There wasn't a single breakthrough moment where everything clicked.

No triumphant cinematic montage where the Fund suddenly became perfect.

There were instead a thousand small, unglamorous wins:

A scholarship approved.

A department saying thank you.

A volunteer re-engaging.

A new officer hearing about us through word of mouth.

A process working the way it was supposed to.

An email from someone who'd been waiting months for help.

A quiet message that said:

"This gave me confidence again."

No fanfare.

No spotlight.

Just life moving forward in ways that mattered.

And each win reinforced a truth I'd been slow to accept:

I wasn't becoming better because I was brave.

I was becoming better because the mission required it.

Purpose does that.

It recruits more of you than you planned to give.

It grows you into someone capable of carrying it.

THE EDGE OF THE MAP

The Fund was never supposed to be about me.

It wasn't about ego or transformation or personal glory.

It was about the people who depended on us —even if they didn't know we existed.

And as the organization grew —slowly, quietly, stubbornly —

I grew with it.

I started making decisions with more breath than panic.

I started trusting myself in moments I used to hesitate.

I started caring less about being impressive and more about being useful.

I didn't feel like a leader.

I didn't feel like an expert.

I didn't feel like someone who belonged in rooms with operators, medics, instructors, or tactical teams.

But I did feel like a protector.

Not the Hollywood kind.

The real kind.

The kind who stays up late making sure the system works.

The kind who carries the mission forward because someone has to.

The kind who honors the people who trusted them —even the ones who never asked.

That was enough.

More than enough.

THE NEXT CHAPTER RISES

Toward the end of this season —after the grief had softened, after the structure had returned, after the small wins had stacked themselves like quiet bricks —a volunteer messaged:

"Hey, you guys going to SHOT Show this year?"

Before this chapter, I would've laughed.

Brush it off as absurd.

Two suburban dads at the largest tactical convention on earth?

Yeah, okay. Sure.

But something inside me didn't laugh this time.

Not because I felt ready.

Not because I thought I belonged.

But because the mission was moving forward —and I was moving with it.

The Fund wasn't fragile anymore.

It was alive.

It was humming.

It was connected.

It was becoming something with gravity —something the world began turning toward rather than away from.

SHOT Show wasn't the end of this chapter.

It was the horizon.

A signal that the world was about to widen in ways I hadn't anticipated.

A reminder that purpose will eventually put you in rooms you never imagined entering —but only if you keep showing up long enough to get there.

BACK HOME DEBRIEF

Service doesn't always wear a uniform.

Sometimes it looks like grief stitched into action.

Sometimes it looks like rebuilding something someone else started.

Sometimes it looks like spreadsheets, emails, and late nights that nobody claps for.

Sometimes it looks like holding the quiet end of the rope while others hold the loud end.

Brandy taught me what quiet leadership looked like.

The Fund taught me what responsibility felt like.

The officers taught me what the stakes really were.

And purpose —the rare kind, the sticky kind —taught me this:

You don't become worthy before you begin.

You become worthy by showing up.

I didn't start this chapter ready.

I didn't start it brave.

I didn't start it with answers.

But I ended it moving toward someone I didn't recognize yet —someone steadier, more accountable, more intentional, more useful.

This chapter wasn't about training.

It was about becoming the man capable of holding what was coming next:

Sheepdog.

D7.

The Mirror Room.

Fear.

Failure.

Insight.

Identity.

And the quiet courage it takes to change.

I didn't know the full scale of what I'd stepped into yet.

I only knew the truth Brandy left behind:

Whatever you do, just keep showing up.

BREAKING POINT

Las Vegas (Henderson), November 2017 — One Month After
Mandalay Bay

The flight into Vegas didn't feel like travel. It felt like an
interruption—like someone pressed pause on my life and
typed in a different scene.

Out the window, the desert looked the same as it always does
from the sky: a sheet of sand sleepwalking toward the
mountains. But when the plane banked and the Strip came
into view, there was a different energy to it. Neon still
burned. Billboards still proposed bad ideas with enthusiasm.
The town never stops selling the illusion that nothing bad
really sticks here.

But some things do.

In baggage claim the slots chirped like wind-up parrots. A
Metro officer stood by the exit doors, arms folded, the kind of
posture that says "this is routine" and the kind of eyes that
say it hasn't been for a while. I'm not an investigator; I don't
know what trauma looks like on paper. I do know what it
looks like in a person who's still showing up.

Jarrod had beat me to the curb. We tossed our bags into an
Uber. The driver tried Vegas small talk, the way locals do
when the town is wildly uninteresting. We passed Mandalay
Bay on the freeway and the car went quiet in the way cars go
quiet when nobody decides to speak first. I stared at the gold
windows and thought about math—angles, distance,
time—and then forced myself to stop. That's not my story to
solve.

Our story was two days long and started in a Jiu Jitsu gym in
Henderson with fluorescent lights that hummed like old bees.
The mats were blue. The room smelled like disinfectant and
courage. Maybe thirty people. Uniforms and T-shirts. Duty
belts set aside with the quiet care of people who know what
they mean. A couple from the country music festival stood

near the back with their hands linked only when no one was looking. New York State Troopers. Vegas Metro, still in it. Civilians, scattered like punctuation. And one New Orleans cop who looked like an apartment building learned how to smile.

We were there because of The Fund. The nonprofit work had turned into real relationships, and those relationships had led to an invitation. Tim Kennedy believes volunteers should train, too. Service without preparedness is just hope with good intentions. We were guests, but we weren't tourists. That mattered, at least to me.

There was a film crew. Not a kid with a phone—shoulder rigs, boom mics, the whole frame. We were told the footage might show up in Sheepdog's online classes. Good. I wanted someone to see what this felt like when the adrenaline wore off. I also didn't especially want my panic memorialized on the internet. You don't get to pick both.

Tim walked in with the cadre. The air shifted the way it does when weather changes. Doc Mike Simpson had the ER calm of a man who's done triage in places with too much noise and too little time. Jeremiah Futch moved easy, like his bones had a blueprint for efficiency. Tim did not take up space the way famous people do. He took up space the way a solution does when it walks into a problem.

He didn't warm us up with a speech. "We train like life depends on it," he said. "Because sometimes it does." No music behind it. No threat. Just a fact set down gently on a table we all recognized.

The rule of Day One was simple: everybody rolls with everybody. No weight classes. No gender lanes. No "I'm a beginner, can I sit this one out?" Everyone pairs. Everyone learns. If you were there, you were in it.

We started moving. Hip escapes. Bridging. Grips. The normal vocabulary of a mat before the grammar gets violent. The mats were clean enough to trust and dirty enough to be honest. I could taste rubber in the air and old sweat from a

173

hundred people who had learned something the hard way in this room.

First roll: civilian about my size. He moved better than I did, which told me he'd rolled before or was lying to himself less efficiently. He caught me with a choke I never saw; I tapped the way pride taps when survival is smarter. We bumped fists. I noticed the camera. I noticed that I noticed the camera. That's a different kind of pressure most people don't talk about: the pressure to be who you think you are in front of a lens that will show who you actually were.

Second roll: different story.

The New Orleans cop stepped forward and we slapped hands. Up close, he was less "apartment building" and more "historical landmark." Forearms like cables. Shoulders like decisions. Kind eyes. The kind that say "I've done bad things so worse things wouldn't happen."

He mounted. His weight settled.

My mind left the room.

It didn't sprint. It leaked. First came the pressure. Then the breath that wasn't enough. Then the edges of my vision folded inward like a book closing on a chapter I hadn't finished. I tried to move the way we were taught. He floated the way only people who've spent a decade getting strangled for fun can float. I bridged. He adjusted. I tried to shrimp and it felt like someone had poured concrete into my hips and told me to swim through the sidewalk.

Panic is not a shout. Panic is a whisper. Panic is your own voice inside your head saying, "You're not getting out," and you believing it because your body is a better storyteller than your courage.

I could hear my heartbeat in my ears, the fluorescent lights above me, the rubber grit against my cheek. I could smell detergent and a metallic hint like an old penny on a tongue.

Somewhere outside of the tunnel someone said "breathe," and I tried, and the breath skipped like a bad CD in an older car. The ceiling blurred. The New Orleans cop said, "You good?" in a voice that wasn't unkind.

I tapped.

He let go instantly. Kind hands. He slid off like someone easing out of a doorway without hitting the jamb. He didn't make it a lesson. He made it a moment. There's a difference.

I sat at the edge of the mat with my back against the wall and remembered every dumb thing I've ever said about staying calm under pressure. Jarrod walked over and handed me water. He didn't tell me to shake it off. He didn't joke. He did that thing friends do when they know the fix is not to say anything clever. He stood there like a piece of furniture you can lean on without breaking it.

Across the room a woman not much over five feet had a man my size pinned and was adjusting grips with the attention of a watchmaker. The couple from the festival moved quiet, consistent, their eyes steady in a way I don't know how to name. A New York trooper took a breath, nodded to his partner, and went again. The room was a chorus of people choosing to continue.

Tim yelled "switch," and the room stirred like water answering gravity. I didn't want to get up. The part of me that likes comfort suggested I wait out one rep and find a "better" time to reengage. Then the woman who'd just finished instructing a man twice her size raised a hand for her next partner and I realized I was not going to be the only person in the room with conditions.

I stood up. Not because I felt brave. Because I felt accountable.

The next rolls were honest. I breathed like Doc Mike told us: in through the nose, hold, out through the mouth. Not performance breath. Maintenance breath. The difference between "try not to die" and "keep thinking." I lost positions

175

and then found them because I stopped talking to myself about how embarrassed I was. Embarrassment is a tax on attention. I couldn't afford it.

Then the drill changed. A blue gun skittered across the mat between two pairs and a dozen conversations ended mid-sentence. Hands changed. Hips changed. Strategies died and were born in the space of one plastic clatter.

We trained that moment over and over: weapons appearing mid-fight, knives dropped from nowhere like math problems handed to kids already taking a test. You think a black belt solves everything until you realize belts don't have magazine capacity. I watched a purple belt with beautiful movement pause one half-second when a knife appeared; the other guy didn't. The match went a different way. Not because of rank. Because of attention.

I learned that day that competition jiu jitsu is a cathedral. Survival jiu jitsu is a storm shelter. The cathedral is beautiful. But when the sirens sound, you should probably know where the shelter is.

The blue guns and knives kept showing up. Sometimes the instructors slipped a blade into your belt without you noticing and yelled "weapon!" so your nervous system could practice choosing to act instead of admire the problem. Hands got clumsy. Eyes got honest. The room got loud the way a room does when polite ends and real starts.

Somewhere in there I rolled with Jarrod. We are good at not turning into comedy when we should be serious, and good at making space for humor when it keeps us moving. He framed. I posted. A training knife clinked, and both of us went feral like two raccoons who'd found the same shiny thing under a porch. He got to it first. I maintain the ref missed something. There was no ref.

The cameras kept moving around us. I'd forget they were there, then remember, and the remembering would try to buy stock in my attention again. I kept telling myself the only

176

documentary that mattered was the one my son would inherit when he watched how I handled myself under pressure.

We broke for water and reset. Tim walked the mat like a carpenter checking corners for square. He corrected small things in ways that moved big ones. Doc Mike watched our faces for the wrong colors and the right breaths. The New Orleans cop gave me a nod from across the room that felt like the exact right thing: not pity, not congratulations, just "I saw you stay."

Afternoon brought the cruelest drill of the day. You're mounted, not winning, not losing, and Tim tosses a knife into your lap like he's dropping change in a jar. The whole world collapses into one problem: who controls the thing that changes everything? Everyone in the room turns into a different version of themselves. Graceful guys get ugly in the best way. Technical guys become practical. The point isn't to be pretty. The point is to be alive.

We cycled that drill until the edges of everything felt sanded. Panic had visited and left forwarding instructions. Breath kept emailing me reminders that it had opinions about my survival. By late afternoon, the part of my brain that quit earlier in the day had rejoined the group with a new attitude.

We circled up. Tim didn't sermonize. "You found your limits today," he said. "Good. Now we train at them." It wasn't forgiveness. It wasn't a dare. It was a map.

The couple who survived the festival squeezed hands once and let go, like they were closing a tab. A Metro officer stared at the mat like it had written him a letter. Jarrod leaned against the wall the way men do when there's nothing left to prove and plenty left to do.

Day Two would be the range. That night would be advanced atmospherics in a Walmart parking lot, which deserves its own chapter because the quiet sometimes teaches louder than gunfire. But the day wasn't quite over. We still had to meet the other half of the curriculum: the hands that would hold the guns.

177

Jeremiah Futch introduced himself like he'd been your friend for years and you'd finally learned his last name. Army Ranger. Three-gun competitor. The way he handled a pistol made me feel like I'd been holding forks wrong my whole life. He spoke in sentences that made mechanics sound like mercy. "Let's get your fundamentals so good the rest of this gets easier." Yes, please.

Then another man stepped up without stepping much at all. Black hair. Beard. Black T-shirt. Gray cargos. A tourniquet sewn into a pocket at the hem like a permanent intention. Sunglasses indoors that somehow didn't look like a costume. No ear pro around his neck. His posture didn't care if you noticed him. Reality does that: it doesn't knock; it just exists.

He said his name was Travis.

He said he'd been in the Army for twenty-five years.

He said North Carolina like someone might take it personally if he didn't include it.

Someone asked about units the way people ask about brands when they don't know how to ask about quality. Travis smiled with his mouth and not his eyes in a way that closed the subject without closing the person. "Been on a couple hundred direct-action hits," he added, like he was mentioning he'd had eggs for breakfast. Not a boast. A weather report.

If you know, you know. If you don't, you don't need to. Either way, the room adjusted.

Jeremiah and Travis are two halves of a whole. One teaches you how to make the gun do what it's supposed to do every single time, even when you're tired and dumb and the sun hates you. The other teaches you that the world will not stand still for your sight picture and that your feet have opinions about your future you've been ignoring.

We weren't on the range yet, but they gave us a primer. Jeremiah ran us through grip theory with the clarity of an engineer who loves clean solutions. Travis watched our hands and then our hips and then the part of our bodies that lives between shots where decisions happen. He didn't correct often. When he did, it was to move a thumb a quarter inch or your weight an inch farther forward and suddenly recoil felt like a conversation instead of an argument.

At one point Travis stepped up to a target and pressed off a string of rounds without ear protection while we stood behind him with ours clamped down tight. Someone pointed it out again, maybe half-joking. He smiled without warmth. "Too late for that decades ago." Not a recommendation. A biography.

Tim stood off to the side, listening the way leaders listen when they trust the room. Even his presence tilted a degree toward Travis, the way gravity nods to larger gravity without needing to explain anything to anyone. It wasn't worship. It was respect among people who know the price tag on competence.

We wrapped the day with logistics for tomorrow. Be on time. Be hydrated. Be honest. Jeremiah said, "You'll do under pressure what you can do without it." Travis added, "You'll do it the way you practiced it." Two sentences I should have had tattooed on my forearms years ago.

We drove back through Henderson while the sun turned the concrete warm enough to remember. Strip malls bled into neighborhoods. A kid rode a scooter past a hedge that was trying to be a wall. I wanted to explain to everyone that the mat today had broken a small piece of me open in a way that felt less like damage and more like surgery. But strangers have their own surgeries scheduled.

Back at the hotel I let the shower fail to erase the mat burn on my cheek. I stood under it until the water was less hot and my thinking was less loud. When I closed my eyes I saw the moment the New Orleans officer's weight shifted from "heavy" to "forever," and I felt again the precise beat when I

179

decided to tap, and again the beat a few hours later when a plastic knife landed between my hips and I did not hesitate. Two decisions made by the same person on the same day. Both honest. One panicked. One present. That difference is the reason to train.

I called home. Logan told me his Lego build wasn't cooperating, which is how seven-year-olds confess to learning patience. I told him I learned how to breathe. He said he already knows how. I told him I'm practicing anyway. He's generous. He said good job, Dad.

Jarrod knocked and came in without waiting because that's what you earn. He tossed me a protein bar. Said we'd earned cheeseburgers but also sleep. He didn't ask about the panic. He didn't need to. We did the very male thing where we sat and watched terrible hotel TV for eleven minutes and then turned it off because there are better silences.

I wrote three lines in a notebook I keep for training and for days when identity needs an audit.

Panic is a language. Learn the grammar.

Weapons change the test, not the lesson.

Breathe first. Then decide.

I've thrown away a hundred notes. I kept that one. It lives in a drawer with other things that hurt and helped.

Morning was coffee and a bagel and a drive to the range with the kind of banter people use to keep the engine from stalling. Jeremiah started us at zero on purpose. Draw. Press. Reset. The discipline of not skipping steps. The humility of being seen doing basics. Every time I wanted to go faster he reminded me that "fast" isn't a speed; it's a side effect.

Travis drifted in like a weather front: not dramatic if you aren't watching, impossible to ignore if you are. Same black shirt. Same beard. Same sunglasses, the kind that make a joke of inside/outside. He watched my feet and said nothing until he did, and then it was only: "Your heels are telling on you." I planted. The gun spoke a new dialect to my hands.

We ran short strings. Jeremiah corrected with small moves that had big consequences. "That thumb is costing you time," he said to a man who was sure speed lived in his trigger finger. Travis adjusted a shooter's stance and then asked him to close his mouth when he breathed. "Decide with air," he said. It sounded dumb until it didn't. Then it sounded like the only way to think.

Across the line the couple from Mandalay Bay shot in a rhythm that didn't apologize for flinches because there were none. They didn't look at each other for reassurance. They looked because that's what you do when you're on the same call. I flinched once at a snap from the next bay and felt ridiculous. My body remembered what it wanted to; their bodies remembered what they chose. There's a difference. I want more of the second.

We shut it down before the light turned weird and people got sloppy. Travis gave us one more line that I wrote in the same notebook: "Reality doesn't care how you feel about your gear." Jeremiah smiled and said, "Or your skill." Not cruelty. Clarity.

On the drive back to the hotel, I counted breath cycles instead of exit signs. In through the nose. Hold. Out through the mouth. The desert outside the window looked less like an afterthought and more like a place with its own rules that you don't get to negotiate with. I thought about the parking lot chapter that would happen that night—the one where noise gets quiet and you realize invisibility is a story you tell yourself to go to sleep. That's for later.

This chapter belongs to the mats.

It belongs to the moment when a man the size of a building reminded me that the human body is a lever system and my brain is the fulcrum that fails first. It belongs to the plastic knives and blue guns that turned technique into choices and

181

choices into futures. It belongs to Doc Mike's steady checks and Tim's short maps and Jeremiah's kind precision and a man named Travis who introduced himself like an answer to a question we were smart enough not to ask out loud.

It belongs to breath.

People love to make "hard to kill" a T-shirt. It's not a shirt. It's a set of habits stacked like sandbags against chaos. Some of those habits look like grip and stance and draw and reload. Some of those habits look like going back to the mat after you shake and tapping when you have to and then not tapping the next time because you created a little space where fear used to sit.

BACK HOME DEBRIEF

This wasn't the day I became tough. It was the day I stopped bargaining with fear.

I learned that panic is not a character flaw. It's a condition. It's data. If you can observe it, you can put structure around it. Breathing is structure. Drills are structure. Friends who hand you water and don't narrate your failure are structure.

The gym gave me a mirror I couldn't avoid. The instructors gave me a language I could actually use. Jeremiah and Travis showed me that competence under pressure is built one boring repetition at a time, and the thing that feels boring today is the thing that will feel like a lifeline tomorrow. Tim and Doc Mike showed me that leadership is pressure you absorb so other people can learn in peace.

I came to Sheepdog because I thought I needed skills. I left understanding I needed responses.

Breathe first.

Then decide.

Then act.

Then repeat.

That's the point of no return.

THE WALMART MINIVAN DEATH SQUAD

Asking your body to be brave is one thing. Asking your brain to stay quiet while you do it is something else entirely.

Day One of Sheepdog Response had already wrung me out like a wet rash guard. I had been mounted by a refrigerator from New Orleans, had a panic attack that felt like a small earthquake inside my ribcage, and spent the rest of the afternoon pretending my hands were not shaking. I told myself the worst was over. That is when Tim said, "Meet us behind the Walmart."

We should have known that was misdirection. It was not behind Walmart. It was right in front—under the humming lights, in plain view of the sliding doors and the late-night crowd of chaos shoppers. Which made it somehow worse. Because hiding in plain sight with thirty men who look like they just crawled out of a Tom Clancy novel is not stealth. It is performance art.

The sun died over Henderson, Nevada, and the world switched to sodium-vapor. We drove out past the last warm-looking restaurant and into a part of town with pawn shops, payday loans, and a sullen pharmacy that looked like it regretted still being open. Jarrod drove the rental. I stared out the window counting how many lights were flickering and how many were just dead. Answer: enough for a horror movie.

The worst Walmart in the zip code sat in a sea of broken asphalt. The kind of lot that has its own weather. We parked in the front where the lamps buzz like angry insects. Two minivans rolled up and slid into the far corner like they were trying not to get noticed. The doors opened and gods climbed out.

Tim. Jeremiah. Futch. Doc Mike Simpson. A guy named Travis who apparently does not need a last name because he moves like a rumor. A handful of other Special Forces dudes in plain clothes. No logos. No bravado. Just the quiet energy of men who have rehearsed danger longer than most of us have held a job.

Minivans. I blinked at them. Soccer-dad chariots. Later someone asked why the minivans and the answer was perfect: room for people, room for gear, decent engines, and nobody looks twice at a minivan. The soccer-dad death squad had arrived, and the world shrugged.

We formed a loose circle under a buzzing lamp. About thirty of us. Civilians, firefighters who paid their own way, a couple off-duty cops, veterans, the whole weird tribe of people who spend weekends trying to become someone worth trusting when it all goes sideways. Tim started talking. I tried to listen.

Then I noticed the shadows moving.

At the edges of the lot, shapes rotated like planets. One near the cart corral. Another by the loading dock. Then gone. I would lock onto an outline for a second and it would dissolve into the kind of normal you never notice until you are trained. They were establishing an unseen perimeter around us, providing overwatch with the subtlety of a magic trick. If you did not know what to look for, you would swear no one was there. If you did, it felt like being guarded by ghosts.

Every instinct in my body screamed to look outward, to watch the approach lanes, to stop the random that always finds a way to wander in—panhandlers, the angry, the drunk, the bored. Twice, people drifted toward us with the curiosity that lives in every American heart: Hey, what is this shady little nightmare meeting under the flickering lamp? I shifted to intercept and Tim just said, without turning, "My guys have it." The shapes flexed, the citizens lost interest, and I tried to turn my brain back toward the lesson while the part of me that likes staying alive had a tantrum.

Tim called it Advanced Atmospherics. It sounded like a college elective you would drop in week two, and it turned out to be the most valuable class I have ever taken. The idea was simple and brutal: learn to read where you are, who is around you, and what the place is trying to tell you, then make decisions before danger grows teeth.

Step one was not "look for bad guys." Step one was macro: understand the zip code. Know the crime trends, the population patterns, the EMS and police response times. Know the radio frequencies. Know where the closest hospital is and how long it takes to get there when the traffic lights are working, and when they are not. Do not just show up—arrive with context.

Step two was atmospherics: the here and now. What is normal in this parking lot at 9:17 p.m. on a Thursday? What does not belong? Who is moving toward you, who is orbiting, who is pretending to shop while watching the group of weirdos under a lamp?

We drifted between cars like ghosts at a drive-in. Not touching—just looking. The longer you do it, the creepier it feels, and the more terrifying it gets. Because you start realizing how much of someone's life is on display through a windshield.

Garage door opener. Company badge. Apartment barcode sticker. The "I Voted" sticker fossilized onto the dash. The "My Kid is an Honor Student at" sticker that tells you exactly which side of town they live on. Add the HOA parking decal, a Starbucks cup with a name, and a gym bag logo—and you have basically written their biography before they ever step outside.

Tim called it out mid-walk. "People think home invasions start at the door," he said. "They start with what you leave in your car."

He was not being dramatic. He was being mathematical.

"You do this over three days," Tim said, tapping the glass of a random sedan, "you build what we call a pattern of life. Every person, every family, has one. You can tell when they leave for work, where they stop for gas, who they love, who they text, and how long they sit at the gym pretending to stretch. Humans are creatures of habit. It gives us comfort. It gives us confidence. But it also makes us painfully, hilariously predictable."

He let that hang in the air like a warning shot. I looked back through the glass at my own reflection and thought about everything sitting in my own front seat back home. Then I thought about selling my truck and riding a bike forever.

Tim did not talk like a mystic. He talked like a mechanic. "Collect data. Build a baseline. Compare against normal. Decide early." He moved car to car, a finger resting on a window without smudging it, calling out details we had not seen and conclusions we had not even known were possible. It was like standing next to a magician who explains the trick and you still cannot see the string.

Then Tim gave the assignment. "Partner up. Go inside. Find someone committing a crime. Do not confront. Do not engage. Do not be weird. Identify the who, what, where, when, how, why. Use your eyes. Use your pattern recognition. Meet back here."

I looked at Jarrod. Jarrod looked at me. We exchanged the universal civilian expression for, "We are absolutely going to be arrested for looking suspicious in Aisle 12." Then we walked toward the automatic doors like we had a reason to live.

The doors sighed open and the bright hum of Walmart swallowed us. If you have never tried to be a ghost in a place built to be loud, it is like trying to whisper underwater. Fluorescents buzzed. Freezers coughed. Carts squealed in long, mournful vowels. My heart rate spiked like I was back on the mat with Big Refrigeration trying to smother me. Stress does not care if there is a trophy at the end. Stress just wants rent.

We took a lap like shoppers. Hold something. Touch something. Do not look like you are hunting people with your eyes. I picked up a bag of chips I did not want, read the back like I was considering the life choices that lead to 35 grams of heart failure, and scanned the reflections in the glass. A couple argued quietly near the pharmacy—volume down, anger up. A teenager in a hoodie drifted with purpose that did not match his empty cart. A man kept checking the ceiling like he owed it money.

The trick, Tim said, was presence without performance. Do not play spy. Just be awake. Notice hands. Notice pace. Notice who looks at exits and who forgets they exist.

We split when the hoodie kid peeled off toward electronics. Jarrod trailed him with the lazy drift of a guy who suddenly remembered he needed a charging cable. I hung back and watched a woman in an oversized coat load cosmetics into the baby seat area and cover them with a flyer. She was a professional. Calm. Efficient. Zero wasted motion. She had done this before.

I felt something twist in my chest. Not judgment. Not heroism. Just the brutal knowledge that people do crimes because life is a set of bad options. My job, tonight, was not to save Walmart from a loss. It was to learn what crime looks like when it is quiet.

I decided to test myself. Not follow her. Track her. Where are her eyes? What is her pattern? What does she check and what does she never look at? She glanced at endcaps, mirrors, other shoppers. Never once at the ceiling. Never at the door cameras. She knew where attention lives and where she could live outside of it. She moved to self-checkout, waited for the line to bulge, then slipped past like a shadow and walked into the night. I let her go. She knew the game. Tonight I learned the rules.

I found Jarrod by the games. The hoodie kid had tucked batteries into his sleeve then changed his mind when a clerk floated near like a friendly shark. He abandoned the plan and bought gum he did not want because that is what survival looks like when your courage is not bigger than your fear.

We came back out into the desert night and the lot felt different. Not safer. Just mapped. The world had gone from impressionistic smear to something with lines. Tim stood where we left him, haloed by the buzz of a dying bulb.

Someone, inevitably, called the cops about a group of scary dudes meeting in the dark and whispering over cars. Henderson PD did not show. Word came down the line that they had done the same class yesterday for the law-enforcement-only version and the watch commander basically said, "Yeah, we know. Tell Tim we said hi." I laughed out loud in that way you do when life is a joke you are glad you get.

That part stuck with me. We were not playing at being part of the world anymore. We were in it. Connected to a network of people who trained in the same way for the same reasons: because when it goes bad, you do not rise to the occasion—you sink to your level of training. I used to think that meant shooting better. Tonight it meant looking better.

Tim closed us out with something I wrote down in my head because it felt like a key. "You are not trying to be paranoid," he said. "You are trying to be early."

Early to notice the car that is parked too close to the cart return with the engine running. Early to note the guy who orbits your family twice without a cart. Early to choose a different aisle. Early to step away. Early to live.

I did not feel brave walking back to the car. I felt... competent. Like someone had handed me glasses and the blur I called life snapped into focus. The fear did not go away. It got organized.

Back Home Debrief:

You do not have to be paranoid. You just have to be awake.

Advanced Atmospherics is not mysticism. It is math. The quiet practice of paying attention to the world before it turns on you. Learn the patterns of your places. Build a baseline. Decide early. Remove the stickers that tell strangers more than they need to know. Park where you can see. Stand where you can move. Watch hands. Trust the part of you that whispers "not today" and leave.

The mat taught me how to survive inside panic. The parking lot taught me how to never meet it in the first place.

And if you ever see a minivan full of men who look like they could remove your skeleton and then hand it back with a protein shake—relax. They are probably just here to teach you how to see.

THE DAY THE LINE PARTED

Vegas smells like brass, beer, and bad decisions. Every hallway hums. Every escalator's jammed with people wearing plate carriers and polos with flag patches. SHOT Show 2018: sixty-five thousand people, sixteen-hundred-plus exhibitors, six-hundred-and-forty-five thousand square feet of tactical capitalism. You don't buy a ticket; you get invited. Military, law enforcement, media—or someone confident enough to fake all three. And somehow, Jarrod and I were on that list.

Two dads from Phoenix who started at a gun-show booth, now walking into the apex of the global arms industry like we belong there. I've got my badge flipped backward, partly from nerves, partly because I don't want anyone asking, "What company are you with?" and hearing me say, "Uh... life experience?"

The first morning hits like sensory concussion. Fluorescents blast off anodized aluminum. Every booth looks like the Death Star gift shop. Jarrod reads the map like he's plotting an assault on the Starbucks line. I'm mostly trying not to sweat through my "business-casual-meets-midlife-crisis" polo and spill hotel coffee on a $4,000 optic.

Every brand we've ever trained with is here—Haley Strategic, Sheepdog Response, Fieldcraft, Crye, 5.11. Influencers film slow-mo reloads next to billion-dollar CEOs shaking hands over drone contracts. It's like walking into the Internet made real—half warrior culture, half dad-bod cosplay, and somehow sincere through all the noise. The wild part? We're professionals now. Our training hours and certifications actually earned us industry credentials. We're not faking it. We just still can't believe it.

We take our first lap. Booth after booth after booth. Antennas, optics, nylon, suppressors, rifles that look like the future and belt buckles that look like they could stop a truck. I'm making mental notes I'll never use: that light is too bright for hallway work; that sling will saw my neck in half; that holster would print like a billboard on a Target run.

Somewhere between the drone cage and a display of "low-profile" plate carriers that could double as winter coats, I realize I haven't exhaled in twenty minutes.

The 5.11 booth is a zoo—hundreds deep. Tim Kennedy is the main attraction, smiling, signing, crushing cans of beer like it's cardio. Jarrod elbows me. "Watch this."

Tim spots us across the crowd. "Hey! It's the brothers!"

He waves us forward—past a hundred people clutching hats and hero worship. We walk up, half-apologizing, half-grinning. Every neck in that line cranes at once: Who the hell are these two? Tim hugs us like old teammates. "You guys made it out here, huh?"

"Yeah," I say, "trying not to get kidnapped by marketing."

He laughs. For a second, we belong.

In a room built on credentials, he gives us something better—recognition. Not as fans. As peers. Then he's back to the line, moving fast, never breaking eye contact with the next person. There's a lesson in that I don't fully get yet.

We drift. We're not hunting autographs. We're hunting proof. Proof that the last few years weren't a fever dream. That the dust and bruises and weird parking-lot drills added up to something. Jarrod grabs a selfie with a trainer we've followed forever—the guy looks exactly like his Instagram and nothing like his Instagram: confident, tired, kind. It's the first time I think, maybe the Internet isn't full of ghosts. Maybe it's just full of people who forget they're people sometimes.

By late afternoon, the edges of the day start to curl. My feet ache in ways that feel like permanent decisions. I've consumed enough caffeine to register as a small earthquake. We call an audible and set up an unofficial hangout at a bar off the convention floor. No banners, no press—just cops, firefighters, a few industry friends, and a bunch of tired people swapping stories over cheap beer. Someone says, "We invited Tim. He'll never show."

Ten minutes later, the door swings open. Tim Kennedy and Nick Palmisciano walk in like a plot twist. The whole table freezes. They don't posture. They just sit, grab beers, and start talking about training, service, and why ordinary people have to stay in the fight. The conversation is loud and weird and human. The kind of night where you meet a K9 handler who gives you a sticker and a sermon. The kind of night where the noise dies down and you realize you're not chasing clout—you're chasing people who care.

I pull a birthday card from my jacket. It's for my wife's grandmother—ninety-nine years old and a die-hard Hunting Hitler fan. "Look, man," I tell Tim, "I've never asked you for anything—and I won't again—but could you sign this for her birthday?"

He grins. "Absolutely." He writes a long, kind note and hands it back like it's nothing.

She framed that card. It stayed on her nightstand until the day she passed. Still the only thing I ever asked Tim for. Still the strangest proof I have that this world and my world can overlap for a second and not tear each other apart.

We step into the hallway under buzzing lights. Jarrod looks at me. "This feels... real."

"Yeah," I say. "That's what scares me."

Next morning, my phone buzzes me awake like an angry drill sergeant. Unknown number: Need you to attend something at 8 a.m. Bring your badge. Can't tell you what it is. No details. Just coordinates. Eight a.m. in Vegas feels like an urban legend. The Strip's still dark, air thick with perfume and regret. I follow Google Maps down an empty side street and stop in front of a nondescript building. No sign—just a sheet of paper taped to the door: Private Event — Brand Summit.

I step inside and freeze.

Gerber. 5.11. Revely Peak Ranch. Half the tactical universe drinking bad coffee like it's jet fuel. Executives, operators, marketing heads. The room smells like coffee and contract money. Tim's at the front, casually commanding the space in jeans and a T-shirt. This isn't a meet-and-greet. It's a closed-door briefing for every brand he partners with—outlining new gear, TV projects, training initiatives, who's building what and why. And me. A suburban dad whose proudest operational achievement is keeping Goldfish crackers out of his rifle bag.

Someone hands me a packet with an NDA stapled to the front. I sign it because everyone else does. My pen squeaks in that way that says, you don't belong here, but we'll allow it.

Tim starts with integrity—how brand loyalty only matters if the gear saves lives, how community beats ego, how the mission dies when the marketing wins. He talks like the instructors who wreck you on day one and hug you on day three. He talks like someone who's tired of pretending he has to impress anyone. And I'm nodding like, Yes, exactly, integrity—that's why I'm sweating through my shirt right now.

Then he shifts. He talks about building bridges between civilians, veterans, and first responders—people who keep showing up when nobody asks them to. He talks about the cost of showing up, and why it's worth it anyway. He looks like he means it. The room looks like it needs to hear it.

Boom moment: it lands.

Because in that instant, I'm not an outsider anymore. I'm sitting in a room full of people who built the world I once watched from a distance, and I'm supposed to be here. I don't know how long that feeling lasts. I just know it's enough to put a crack in the old story I've been telling myself about who belongs.

They roll a preview of his Discovery Channel show. Explosions, training montages, hero shots. Everyone claps politely. I'm trying not to cry. For years I looked at these people like demigods. Now I'm part of the conversation. Not the loudest voice in the room or the most important—just a voice that wasn't there before.

When it ends, Tim walks the room shaking hands. He spots me near the back. "Glad you could make it, brother." Then he's gone, swallowed by suits and operators. I stand there for a second, letting it sink in. The fluorescent lights buzz overhead like applause that doesn't know when to stop.

Jarrod's waiting outside with two coffees. "How'd it go?"

"You ever walk into a meeting and realize you're the only one who didn't bring a multimillion-dollar contract?"

He grins. "So... good meeting then?"

We walk back toward the convention center, two nobodies with VIP badges, trying not to look as stunned as we feel. The floor looks different now. Not smaller. Just... navigable. Like I could find the exits on purpose.

That night we end up at the infamous Frogman After-Party—a blur of whiskey, war stories, and tactical celebrity sightings. Music is loud enough to vibrate bone. Someone's telling a story about a parachute that refused to open until it was threatened. Some Florida SWAT breacher corners me to talk door charges. We're deep into hinge geometry and overpressure angles, trading notes like old colleagues. Halfway through, he squints. "You military?"

"Nope. Dad of two. Great with glue guns, though."

He stares, then laughs, maybe thinking I'm kidding. I'm not. That laugh is the last bit of imposter syndrome leaving my body.

Vegas is full of caricatures—the operator, the brand guy, the fanboy, the troll. But tonight, nobody's playing the trope. It's just people who've done hard things or want to, hanging out near a bar that smells like spilled courage. It hits me that our weird little journey—from a Phoenix gun show to a rappel tower to a Walmart parking lot—somehow deposited us right in the middle of this. And nobody's asking for our paperwork.

By the last morning, I can finally hear my own thoughts over the buzz. We loop the floor again with less urgency. I shake hands I won't wash for a bit. We skip the lines that don't matter and find the conversations that do—the small brands making good gear for the right reasons; the quiet guys who teach without selling you shame; the women who've been carrying the logistics of this whole scene while the rest of us chest-bumped about it online. The circus is still the circus. I'm just not juggling anymore.

We sit on the edge of the convention center with our backs against a wall of concrete and glass. Our knees hurt. Our phones are dying. Jarrod scrolls our photos—blurry, perfect, real. I thumb the corner of that birthday card envelope like it's a talisman. It feels like proof that I was here and also proof that I wasn't the point.

We talk about the Brand Summit more than anything. How strange it felt to sit in that room—how convicted I felt hearing someone say out loud that all this gear means nothing if it doesn't save lives. It reorders things. It puts the shiny objects back in the display case and pulls the people to the front of the shelf.

On the flight home, I watch Vegas shrink into a geometry of lights and wrong turns. I think about the hug at the 5.11 booth, the handshake at the Brand Summit, the laugh at the party. None of them are tactics. None of them would make a cool range video. But each one chipped away at the wall between them and us until there wasn't a wall anymore—just a room full of people trying to get better without pretending they're invincible.

BACK HOME DEBRIEF:

SHOT Show was supposed to be a field trip. It became a rite of passage. We'd trained for years to be competent. Now we were accepted. Not because we were special—but because we kept showing up.

Belonging didn't arrive as a medal or a follower count. It snuck up as a hug in public, a seat at a table I didn't know existed, and a breacher's laugh I wasn't sure I'd earned. It reminded me that being "hard to kill" isn't about flexing—it's about finally standing still long enough to see who's standing with you.

Next up is the part no one posts—the part where the lights go down and the pressure goes up. But that's why this chapter matters. It's the breath before the plunge. The warmth you carry into the cold. The reminder that when the simulator knocks the wind out of you, there's a reason to get back up that isn't ego.

You get one hug, one handshake, one laugh—and then you go do the work.

THE ROOM THAT KNOWS YOU

My wife handed me the envelope like it was a love letter or a court summons—something that would change things either way.

"Go," she said. "You need this."

Inside was a certificate to D7 at Haley Strategic.

I laughed, because laughter is what you do when your stomach drops. D7 had always lived on the horizon in my head—north star stuff. The place you point to when you're still building yourself in the dark. We'd joked about it after Marauders, after Sheepdog. One day. When I'm actually ready.

197

I wasn't ready. But I went anyway.

I went alone.

No Jarrod. No familiar face to crack a joke with on the drive or nudge me back into my body when I floated away. Just me, a thermos of bad coffee, and the long, quiet stretch of highway into Scottsdale that always feels like it's shrinking the closer you get to the city.

The building doesn't look like a gun range. It looks like a rehab clinic for elite athletes—white walls and clean lines and cameras where you don't expect cameras. The lobby smells like disinfectant and new rubber. There's a Brock string hanging from a rig in the corner. Someone is balancing on a physio ball, pistol unloaded, sight picture steady, jaw loose. A trainer cues cadence with a metronome and a soft voice.

And the thing that makes my neck hairs stand up: the stillness. Not the quiet—lots of places are quiet. The stillness. The way the air feels when it's being watched.

"Welcome," the man at the desk says.

I nod, sign the waiver that includes the words force feedback, and pretend I'm not reading them twice.

I've done hard. I've done confusing. I've done chaos under smoke and men twice my size trying to choke me with their bones. This is different. This is surgical.

We get the orientation—gas blocks, cadence drills, what they call cognitive load. We talk decision fatigue. Reaction time. Why a quarter-second isn't just a number—it's a picture you're late to.

I do the Brock string. My eyes fight each other like they're on separate teams. I'm already sweating.

Someone points me to a station with slow-motion replay. I fire a short string. Then I watch it back. There's the micro-flinch I swear I didn't feel. There's the grip pressure leaking to my thumbs. There's my breath, which apparently forgot it had a job.

Notes. Adjustments. More notes.

The whole thing isn't designed to make you feel good. It's designed to tell the truth.

We cycle through stations until the room shifts. They dim the outer lights. A door opens that looks like part of the wall. And there it is.

The simulator.

It's not a screen; it's a world. 270 degrees of high-def reality that hates you a little. The floor is grippy. The ceiling hums. Speakers breathe behind you. A trainer fits the vest to my torso and tightens it one click past comfortable. The cable at my spine is heavier than I expected. Not heavy like weight—heavy like consequence.

"Confirm trigger discipline," he says. "Confirm safe direction. Confirm you're hydrated."

"Confirmed," I say. I don't sound like me.

They hand me a training pistol that snaps and points and locks back like the real thing. My hands know what to do. My brain does not.

"Look center," the voice says in my headset. "Find neutral. Keep your breath quiet. Scenario loads in five."

The room goes black, then it blooms.

A street. Asphalt glinting. Late light. Kids on a motorbike weave too close to a sedan. The sedan stops. The driver gets out, yelling. I move without thinking. The bike wobbles; the passenger reaches into a backpack.

Tunnel vision roars in like a wave. The sound thins and stretches. My hands move on their own.

Two steps. Verbal. Angle. Decision.

Press. Press. Press.

The room snaps to white. The screen freezes. The sound dies like someone closed a door.

"What happened?" I say. My throat is dry.

"Don't leave yet," the trainer says. "Watch."

We run it back in slow motion. My shots are clean staggered hits. The angle is better than I thought. I said the words I was supposed to say. I didn't flag anyone. I didn't choke.

"Good work," the trainer says, and the words land like ice on a burn.

I breathe. I unclench. I feel the part of me that still wants to be chosen start to warm up like a dog coming when you call.

That's when D7 does what D7 does.

They don't high-five you. They don't let you go bask in a corner with your water bottle and post about it.

"Reload," the voice says. "Scenario two in ten."

The world appears again. An ATM camera angle. Stucco walls. Desert landscaping. The kind of streetlight we have on our block. My brain registers the colors before it registers the threat. The tan of the building is the tan from my grocery store. The ocotillo in the background might as well be my neighbor's yard. There's the green glare on the glass, the kind of reflection your eyes jump to when your kid stands in front of it and makes faces.

My heart rate spools like a winch.

A man walks up behind the woman at the ATM. He's too close. I move left to get an angle and smash into the side of the world I can't see—the edge of the projection that feels like air until you meet it. My breath is too loud in my own head. The world flickers sharper, then smaller. The man turns, the woman turns, they both talk at once, and the framing suddenly compresses like someone shoved me into a closet.

I hesitate.

It is the most human thing I do.

The vest bites down with a sudden, angry hiss.

It isn't pain, not like breaking something. It's pain the way shame is pain—the kind that puts hot hands on your ribs from the inside and asks how much you really want to be here.

"Reset," the voice says. Calm. Not unkind.

I step out of the box, and my legs don't care for it. I sit. I stand. I pretend I'm stretching. I pretend it's fine.

"Hydrate," another trainer says. He isn't smiling. He isn't frowning. He's a flat line. The kind of flat line you get from people who don't need to perform their competence.

"Scenario three in thirty," the headset whispers.

"No," I think. "Please not yet."

"Load," the headset says.

A front door cracked open. A baby carrier on the couch. Sun-bleached yard. Air that looks like it smells like heat. I know this house. Not literally, but I know this house. Everyone in this part of Arizona knows this house. My eyes pick a thousand useless details: the gap in the blinds, the scuff on the baseboard by the hinge, the cheap rug from a big-box store that trips you when you're carrying groceries.

A figure moves and a voice rises from a back room. The hallway is narrow in the way cheap houses are narrow—a design that turns men into battering rams. My muzzle floats between two frames, and I make the worst decision you can make: I try to make a better decision.

The vest hits me again. Harder this time, because my brain is ready and my body isn't.

"Out," the voice says. Not a command. A boundary.

I get to a bathroom without remembering how. The tile is too clean, and somehow that pisses me off. I sit on the lid of a toilet like a man hiding from bad news. I drink water I can't taste. I guarantee the guy in the mirror that I am fine. The guy in the mirror looks unconvinced.

There's a knock. Not on the door—on the space I'm taking up.

"You good?" the trainer asks from the hallway.

"No," I say. It slips out. The truth always does when your breath is wrong.

"Okay," he says. "Want back in?"

I don't. Not even a little.

"Yes," I say, because that's the whole point of all of this, isn't it? Not wanting to and doing it anyway.

The hallway back to the sim box is shorter now. The walls walk with me. Someone clips the vest back on and it feels like agreement.

"Check heart rate," the trainer says. He glances at my wrist, then at my eyes. "Maybe sit after this one."

"Am I going to die?" I say, too soft.

"Maybe," he says, even softer. "Who's next after you?"

The room appears.

Office lobby. Glass. Polished floor. The kind of place you bring a resume and a lie about how much you like working with teams. People move with the confidence of civilians—oblivious and beautiful. Something in a reflection moves opposite. The angle is bad, the echo is worse, and I'm already two choices behind by the time they line up.

I make the wrong one.

The vest hits me, and the shame isn't electric anymore—just heavy. Like a wet coat I deserve.

They stop me. They don't let me play hero. D7 is merciful in the cruel way a mirror is merciful—it refuses to lie, and that saves you.

We debrief without adjectives. We watch the tape. They talk about eye speed, about when my attention shifted before my body did, about the exact half-second where I decided to make the perfect shot instead of the right one.

"Good mechanics," one trainer says. "But you're letting your mind go places your body can't follow."

"Story of my life," I say, and he doesn't smile.

I spend the rest of day one doing smaller drills that feel like penance. Cadence. Decision trees. Verbal. No-shoots. My hands remember. My head starts to. We finish with a talk from Haley himself.

If you don't know him, it's easy to imagine the caricature: the warfighter, the legend. That's not what walks into the room. What walks in is a man who looks like he's spent a lot of years listening to people talk about fear and then trying to build them a bridge across it. He doesn't posture. He asks questions that make you realize your answers were never answers at all—just noises you made to feel safe.

He talks about performance under stress, about how cognitive load amputates nuance. About breath. About focal planes. About being honest when your nervous system writes checks your identity can't cash.

And then he leaves us with something infuriatingly simple:

"You can't fake who you are under pressure."

I go home quiet. The sun is going down behind the McDowells, turning the whole valley into a bruise. I feel hollowed and scrubbed. The boys are in the kitchen building a fort out of chairs and blankets. My wife looks at me like she's trying to read a scan. I kiss her forehead and say, "Thank you." She nods like she knew that's what today was all for.

I don't sleep well. The house clicks and settles and every click is a scenario loading. I hate it. I love it. I want to quit. I can't.

Day two is the same building with different light. Morning makes everything look more honest. The lobby coffee is worse, which somehow comforts me. I stretch. I do my drills. I don't try to impress anyone with how not-shaky my hands are.

"Back in the box," the voice says.

The vest is easier this time, not because it's looser but because I don't argue with it.

We start with a simple task that isn't simple: look where you don't want to. Then we compound it: speak when you don't want to. Then we make it ugly: move when you don't want to.

Scenario loads. City sidewalk. The framing is busy on purpose. I pick the wrong thing to ignore and the right thing to follow. It's a small win. No vest. No applause.

We stack decisions like coins. I can feel when my eyes shift too late now. That's new. The tunnel vision still punches the edges of the world, but I can feel where the tunnel begins instead of just waking up inside it.

Another scenario. This one wants me to commit too soon. I don't. I hate how proud I am of that. I say the words. I adjust my angle. A trainer whispers, "There." I don't know if he means do it or almost. I do it anyway.

We break. Heart rate checks. Someone hands me a protein bar like a sacrament. Someone else cues breathing and watches my shoulders like a hawk.

No big speeches. No "look at you now." D7 is a museum of what you actually are. Some exhibits are closed for renovation. Some are nothing but ash-colored walls with a sign that says *Here we will build a thing when you stop lying to us.*

We finish on drill work that would look boring on video. It is not boring. It is where the growth hides. The slow-mo shows fewer micro-flinches. My front sight doesn't wobble like a guilty tell. My hands and eyes sign a truce.

Haley gathers us for a final brief. He doesn't tell stories to make himself taller. He reminds us that the real fight is never the one you imagined, and that most of life is the hour before anything happens.

He says, "Get curious about your stress. The moment you judge it, you stop learning."

Someone asks about tactics. He nods at the room, at the cameras, at the vest, at the quiet.

"Those are tactics," he says. "For your mind."

We clap, because we're civilians and clapping is how we tell ourselves it's okay to leave.

I drive home on side streets, not because I'm paranoid but because I want to see the stupid details I always miss—the mailbox with the dent, the shopping cart abandoned in the median, the way the afternoon breeze sneaks under the edges of a sunshade on a minivan and makes it breathe like a sleeping thing.

I pull into my driveway and sit with the engine off. The house stares at me with my own windows. A neighbor waves. I wave back and wonder how many scenarios would pass for normal if you weren't looking.

That night, I walk the perimeter of my home the way you do when you've seen a ghost. Not because I think anything is coming. Because the point of D7 was never the attack. The point was the space inside me that always chooses what to see.

I stand in the hallway where the rug catches your boot heel if you're carrying too much. I stand in the kitchen where the back door swallows sound. I stand in the living room and look at the baby photos we still haven't rotated out of frames. The house is the house. The world is the world. I am the thing that's different.

On Monday, a coworker asks how my "gun class" went. I say, "Fine." Then I make a spreadsheet I should've made six months ago. Then I text my wife to ask what time she wants me home. Then I pull a sticker off my car because maybe the smallest signals are the loudest.

There's a version of this story where I tell you I came out sharper, faster, deadlier. That would be a lie told by the kind of guy I don't want to be anymore.

I came out slower.

And slower, for me, is the miracle.

Slower to assume. Slower to decide I'm the hero. Slower to pick the perfect shot over the right action. Slower to let my fear sprint ahead and narrate.

206

The week after D7, a stranger swerves into my lane and slams his brakes. The old tape starts—heart rate, heat, a dumb story about face and fairness. But I hear it now. I watch the tunnel try to build itself.

I blink long, twice. I breathe through my nose. My hands feel the wheel like it's a question.

I let him go.

It feels like losing. It feels like winning. It feels like what I came to learn in the first place: you don't train to be a warrior in a movie. You train to be a father who comes home.

BACK HOME DEBRIEF

D7 didn't make me look cool. It made me honest.

I went in thinking it was about skill. It was about control—the kind you practice when nothing is happening so that when everything is happening, some calm part of you remains in charge.

I thought I'd be judged on mechanics. I was judged on whether I could stay present when my brain screamed for shortcuts.

I wanted to be faster. I learned to be slower.

The simulator didn't show me monsters I haven't met yet; it showed me how I turn ordinary rooms into monsters when I'm scared.

It used Arizona against me—my colors, my stucco, my little life—and reminded me I will never be fighting "out there." I will always be fighting in here.

My wife asked me, later, if it was worth it. I told her the truth: it was horrible. And it changed me.

You can't fake who you are under pressure. You can only practice who you'll be when it shows up.

So that's the plan now. Less performing. More practice. Less noise. More breath.

Slower. Truer. Harder to kill in the ways that matter.

WHEN THE NOISE STOPS

You don't really understand what training has done to you
until the noise stops.

Not the gunfire.

Not the alarms.

Not the screaming role-players.

I mean the internal noise—the churn in your gut that keeps
you chasing harder courses, harder instructors, harder proof.
Somewhere after D7, when the bruises faded and the
adrenaline drained out of my bloodstream, the quiet finally
caught up with me.

And that's when the real work began.

I would sit at my desk after the kids went to bed, the house
still and dark, staring at the certificates on the wall like they
were crime scene photos. Not trophies. Not souvenirs. Just a
lineup of moments where the world asked something of
me—and I either stepped up or I didn't.

Each one was a scar I chose.

Each one was a turning point.

Each one was a version of myself I had to contend with.

It wasn't pride I felt. It wasn't nostalgia.

It was weight.

The weight of becoming someone I didn't recognize at first,
then couldn't deny.

The friends who don't stay.

People don't tell you that getting better comes with a body count.

Not literal.

Social.

When I first started training, I assumed life would continue in parallel—same friends, same routines, same level of comfort, plus a few new skills I could lean on when things went sideways. What I didn't expect was the slow orbit-shift of the people around me.

At first, it was subtle.

A couple of jokes about "midlife crisis commando school."

A few cancelled plans.

A weird distance I couldn't name.

Then the group chat got quiet.

Then the invitations dried up.

Then the calls stopped coming.

No drama. No conflict. They just... slipped away.

When you start changing your relationship with fear, discipline, and responsibility, the people who aren't ready for that change start to feel judged—even when you're not judging anyone. You're simply moving. You're tightening your life. You're choosing deliberate over comfortable.

But growth is subtraction before it's addition.

And losing people you thought were permanent is the tax.

I didn't understand that then.

I do now.

Fearless to a Fault

There's a phrase I picked up somewhere between the breaching tower and the night shoot: fearless to a fault.

People hear that and think it's bravado.

It isn't.

What it really means is:

When you've rehearsed chaos enough times, fear stops being prophecy and becomes information.

That's the shift training makes that nobody talks about. Before all this, danger lived in the corners of my mind like an unlit hallway. Every noise in the night. Every stranger in the parking lot. Every story on the news.

After training?

Threats didn't evaporate.

They just started making sense.

Chaos became solvable instead of existential.

Stress became data instead of doom.

Fear became a speed bump instead of a stop sign.

When an internal storm hits and you've been breathing through scenarios that make normal life look like recess, you stop wishing the world were easier. You start trusting that you're capable.

Too capable, sometimes.

Calm under pressure is intimidating to people who haven't had to earn it. In one job, that calm read as defiance. My boss didn't want someone who could think for himself. He wanted someone who looked rattled when he did. When I didn't mirror his panic, he saw it as insubordination.

He made sure I left.

And weirdly?

It was a relief.

If your competence threatens someone, you're in the wrong room.

Training didn't cost me that job.

It revealed that I'd outgrown it.

The Family Parallel

If you want to know the real gift of training, don't look at the range.

Look at a kitchen at 3:00 a.m.

Crying toddler.

Dishes in the sink.

Sleep-deprived frustration simmering under the surface.

That's the real battlefield.

Working through chaos on purpose gave me the ability to handle chaos at home without becoming part of the problem. When you've had to think clearly under a strobe of smoke, noise, and stress, a tantrum doesn't feel like a threat—it feels like a situation. And situations can be handled.

Our household used to feel like improvisation.

After training, it felt like a plan.

Dinner at this time.

Bedtime at that time.

Routines that didn't change because I didn't feel like following them that day.

People hear "discipline" and think military coldness.

They're wrong.

Discipline is compassion dressed as consistency.

It gave my kids predictability. It gave my wife partnership. It gave me clarity. And on the days we slipped—and we did—it gave us a roadmap back to center.

I didn't become a drill sergeant.

I became a man my family didn't have to worry about.

Training didn't harden me.

It sharpened me.

The fog that finally lifted

Before training, danger was blurry.

Everything felt like it could be "the thing."

The wrong car.

The wrong noise.

The wrong moment.

213

D7 stripped that illusion away.

When you've been thrown into high-definition simulations designed to overwhelm your senses and expose your blind spots, you come out seeing the world more clearly than you ever did.

Not as a battlefield.

As a map.

Patterns.

Signals.

Terrain.

Most people live in "worst-case scenario" fear because they don't know what their options are. They've never tested themselves under pressure. They don't know what their mind will do.

I do.

That doesn't make me better.

It makes me responsible.

Why the certificates stay up

The certificates in my office aren't decorations.

They're reminders.

A ledger of lessons paid for in sweat, panic, humility, and clarity.

Each one hangs level and straight because someday my sons will take them down. Maybe tomorrow. Maybe in a decade. Maybe long after I'm gone.

If I'm still here when they ask why I did all this, I'll tell them the truth:

I wasn't training to look dangerous.

I was training to be dependable.

Those courses weren't about image.

They were about readiness—for the fire, for the fall, for the unexpected Wednesday afternoon when everything goes wrong at the same time.

I trained so I could be enough.

For them.

For my wife.

For the strangers I might one day need to help.

For the version of myself I used to be.

Those certificates aren't proof of capability.

They're proof of commitment.

What I actually got out of all this

If you strip away the gear, the dust, the screaming instructors, the bruises, the panic attacks, the breakthroughs...

What remains is simple:

Clarity.

Capacity.

Calm.

Not cool-guy swagger.

Not hero fantasies.

Not ego.

Training didn't turn me into a warrior.

It turned me into someone my family could count on.

Useful when things break.

Useful when someone panics.

Useful when a moment requires action instead of fear.

Useful when it's time to breathe instead of react.

Useful when the people I love need steadiness, not noise.

When people say they'd die for their family, they usually mean it.

But training taught me something more important:

Dying for them is easy.

Living for them—showing up, being present, being prepared—that's the actual work.

And that work doesn't end.

It evolves.

BACK HOME DEBRIEF

Doing hard things has a half-life.

It follows you home.

It shapes your tone, your patience, your systems, your sense of what matters.

It forces you to stop being the man you were comfortable being and start being the man your family actually needs.

Training didn't give me a new identity.

It removed the wrong one.

It left behind someone quieter.

More deliberate.

Less ruled by fear.

More anchored in presence.

Less interested in looking capable,

and more interested in being it.

This chapter isn't a victory lap.

It's a reminder:

Transformation isn't the moment you conquer something.

It's the moment you realize you can't go back.

And I won't.

Not now that I've seen who I can be when the noise stops

and the real work begins.

READY IS A WAY OF LIFE

There's a strange kind of silence that hits after you've gone through enough chaos on purpose. It isn't peace. It isn't relief. It's something closer to calibration—like your brain is finally running the right software for the life you already have.

After D7, after the panic, after the mirror, after the clarity, I found myself walking around my own house like it was new terrain. The same hallways. The same kitchen. The same backyard. But I wasn't moving through them as the same man.

The question that finally landed wasn't dramatic.

It wasn't tactical.

It wasn't even complicated.

"Now what?"

Not what's the next course.

Not what's the next challenge.

Not what skill am I still missing.

Just:

How do I live this out?

How do I build a life aligned with the man I've become?

How do I make sure all of this actually matters?

That's the plan.

Not a gear list.

Not a loadout.

Not a fantasy.

A blueprint.

A way to live that keeps you ready in the moments that count and calm in the moments that don't.

It's simple, but not small.

And it applies to anyone—even if your bang to boom has nothing to do with breach points or stress houses.

This is what "hard to kill" means.

1. Start Where You Actually Stand

Most people plan for emergencies they saw on TV, not the ones sitting quietly in their real lives.

You're more likely to face:

- a medical issue

- a lost kid

- a crisis at home

- a panic moment

- a tough conversation

- a broken system

- a split-second decision you didn't train for

...than you are a carjacking or a home invasion.

Your life already has enough real danger baked into it.

So start where you stand:

Your kitchen.

Your driveway.

Your routines.

Your weaknesses.

Your blind spots.

Your temperament on a bad day.

Your ability to think when you're exhausted.

That's your arena.

If you can handle that well, you're already ahead of 99% of people.

2. Clarity Beats Gear Every Time

Before training, everything looked like a threat.

After training, everything looked like a process.

That's clarity.

And clarity is the single most underrated skill you can develop.

Clear people think first.

Clear people breathe first.

Clear people don't rush into the wrong door.

Clear people don't mistake fear for fact.

Clear people don't become part of the problem.

If you want to be a skilled good guy, start with clarity.

And clarity starts with honesty:

Where do I fall apart?

When do I panic?

What do I avoid?

What do I not know?

Gear is a distraction until clarity exists.

Once you're clear, gear just becomes a tool—not an identity.

3. Build Your System Backwards

Most people build preparedness forward:

Gear → Skill → Scenario → Mindset.

That's backwards.

The correct order is:

1. Scenario

What actually scares you? Identify it. Name it. Own it.

Not the cool one—the honest one.

2. Mindset

Who do you need to be in that moment?

Calm? Decisive? Observant? Protective?

222

3. Skill

What would you need to know?

Medical? Communication? Movement? Breath control?

4. Tool

What gear supports that skill, in that mindset, for that scenario?

Now you're building a life—not just a kit.

4. The Ordinary Reps Are What Save You

People romanticize emergency situations.

They don't romanticize:

- grabbing the right drawer in the dark

- remembering which kid sleeps lightly

- shutting the oven off without thinking

- dialing 911 without fumbling

- keeping your voice steady

- helping someone breathe

- getting your family out of the house

- turning chaos into choreography in two seconds flat

These don't look heroic.

They look boring.

Boring is good.

Boring is repeatable.

Boring shows up when adrenaline tries to delete your brain.

If you want to be a protector, practice boring things until they become instinct.

Boring saves lives.

5. The Two-Minute Rule

Here's the rule I live by now:

If I can do it calmly in two minutes, I can do it under stress.

If I can't, I won't.

Two minutes to find a flashlight.

Two minutes to close out a kitchen.

Two minutes to stabilize a bleeding cut.

Two minutes to calm a kid.

Two minutes to assess a room.

Two minutes to breathe through the shakes.

If you want to test yourself, don't go to a range.

Try navigating your own house at 3 a.m. without turning on every light.

That'll show you who you are.

6. The Breath Is the Bridge

Of all the things I learned—under pressure, under panic, under a taser—the breath is the one that stayed.

Because when your breath goes, your thoughts go.

When your thoughts go, your decisions go.

And when your decisions go, your life belongs to whatever scared you.

But if you can get your breath back?

You get everything back.

Slow inhale.

Hold.

Longer exhale.

Reset.

Reboot.

Re-engage.

The breath is the bridge between fear and clarity.

Between panic and presence.

Between who you were and who you're trying to become.

If you take nothing else from this book, take that.

7. Your Bang to Boom Is Your Own

People assume this is a tactical book.

It isn't.

This is a book about what happens when you choose to step toward the thing that scares you—whatever that thing is.

Your bang might be:

- your first therapy session

- your first honest conversation

- your first boundary

- your first attempt at sobriety

- your first failure you didn't run from

- your first real look in the mirror

Your boom might be the fallout from that courage.

Your breath is the moment you realize what it all means.

You don't need to train like I did.

You don't need to run in moon dust or taste adrenal fog or step into a scenario house.

You just need your version of hard.

Your version of forward.

Your version of responsibility.

And you need the courage to breathe through it.

That's what starts the transformation.

That's what keeps it going.

8. The First Promise Every Protector Makes

There's one promise that sits underneath everything I learned.

It isn't fancy.

It isn't dramatic.

It's this:

Show up.

Not perfectly.

Not fearlessly.

Not with the right answer every time.

Just show up.

Show up for your responsibilities.

Show up for your people.

Show up for yourself.

Show up even when you're scared.

Show up even when you're tired.

Show up even when the old version of you tries to drag you back.

You don't rise to the occasion.

You fall to your level of preparation.

So prepare with intention.

Live with clarity.

Speak with presence.

Move with purpose.

227

And breathe—

always breathe.

BACK HOME DEBRIEF

Being "hard to kill" is not about turning yourself into a weapon.

It's about becoming someone your family can rely on.

Someone who thinks clearly.

Someone who breathes through panic.

Someone who doesn't freeze.

Someone who doesn't escalate.

Someone whose presence calms the room.

Someone who keeps the blind spots small.

Someone who has a plan—not out of fear, but out of love.

This book was never about turning civilians into commandos.

It was about turning men into protectors, parents into anchors, and ordinary people into the kind of humans who can be trusted when the moment tilts sideways.

This isn't a manual.

It's a map.

Take what you need.

Leave what you don't.

Write your own bang to boom.

Honor your own breath.

Build your own plan.

And when the moment comes—

and it will—

remember this:

Readiness is how we love the people who depend on us

before the crisis ever arrives.

No bragging.

No theatrics.

No hero costume.

Just one honest promise:

Next time it matters...

I'll be ready.

EPILOGUE — THE NOD

San Jose wasn't supposed to matter. It was supposed to be a corporate off-site—the kind where adults in branded fleece vests debate "alignment" while drinking coffee that tastes like printer toner. A bubble-wrapped retreat from consequence. A theme park for people whose emergencies live in Slack channels.

My coworker crushed his cigarette and said he'd see me inside.

But I stayed.

Not because anything looked wrong.

Not because I felt brave.

Just because something deep inside me—the same thing the desert hammered into me, the mats squeezed out of me, the simulator shocked into me—whispered: Wait.

So I did.

I scanned the world the way I do now.

Not dramatic.

Not tactical.

Just awake.

Condition Yellow.

Most people live their whole lives in Condition White—heads down, phones up, drifting half-present through routines that feel safe because nothing's challenged them yet.

It's not weakness.

230

It's not a flaw.

It's human.

But here's the thing no one likes to admit:

If you're surprised in Condition White,

you're already behind.

That day, I wasn't behind.

I saw the squad car first.

Parked quietly.

Watching the world breathe.

Then the building doors opened and a small female officer stepped outside, wrestling a suspect twice her size and three times her anger.

He was lightning trapped in a human shape—charged, restless, waiting for the moment to blow.

I didn't puff up.

Didn't step in.

Didn't try to be the hero of someone else's story.

I just slid my backpack behind a trash can—clearing space before space mattered.

Not bravado.

Not paranoia.

Just presence.

And then the world shifted.

Everything slowed.

Everything stretched.

Everything gathered into a single, suspended inhale.

THE BREATH BEFORE

There is a moment before violence—a thin, stretched-out, delicate moment—when the world takes one long inhale and waits to see what you're made of.

That's the breath before.

And I felt it hit.

The suspect's shoulders twitched—tiny, almost nothing—but in the breath before, the smallest movements explode with meaning.

FRAME 1 — THE HEAD TURN

His chin snapped left. Micro-movement. But micro is where chaos begins.

FRAME 2 — THE ARM TIGHTENING

His biceps flexed—the universal signal for:

"I'm about to make this everybody's problem."

232

FRAME 3 — THE SHIFT

His heel lifted.

Violence lives in the heel.

Left means she loses balance.

Right exposes her holster.

Back means shattered glass.

Forward means crushed cartilage.

FRAME 4 — THE HANDS

His fingers flared open.

Hands speak before people do.

Hers tightened.

Mine did too.

FRAME 5 — THE ENVIRONMENT

The curb.

The bench.

The window.

The bumper.

The sidewalk.

233

Every surface here was a blunt-force injury waiting for momentum.

FRAME 6 — HER MATH

She was running calculus at light speed:

- "If he slips, do I chase?"

- "Where are his hands?"

- "Where is my gun?"

- "Where is backup?"

She didn't know it was seconds away.

All she knew was that she was alone.

FRAME 7 — THE COIL

His spine compressed—the pre-strike moment.

The breath before tightened around all three of us.

FRAME 8 — BACKUP ARRIVES

The second cruiser rolled up quietly—urgency without panic.

The officer stepped out—large, calm, carved from experience.

He didn't need time.

He didn't need context.

He didn't need the story.

The breath before had already told him everything.

He saw:

- the shoulder tension

- the torque in the hips

- her compromised leverage

- the suspect's vector

- my posture

- the environment

- every hazard

- every outcome

And he moved.

No words.

No hesitation.

No noise.

Just clean, trained intervention.

He clamped the suspect, rotated his body, drove him into the cruiser, and slammed the door.

The breath before exhaled.

Time snapped back.

The moment dissolved.

And suddenly...

nothing happened.

No strikes.

No gun grabs.

No broken glass.

No injuries.

No tragedy.

Just silence.

The kind you only get when danger almost grew teeth—but
didn't.

THE RELEASE VALVE: THE NOD

Then the officer turned.

Not past me.

Not through me.

At me.

And he nodded.
Slow.

Deliberate.

Heavy with recognition.

Not gratitude.

Not warning.

Not territorial.

Recognition.

A silent acknowledgment from one man living in condition yellow to another.

He saw the way my stance shifted.

The way I watched hands, not faces.

The way my weight settled.

The way I prepared without performing.

He saw experience.

He saw readiness.

He saw a man who no longer lives in Condition White.

A man who doesn't pretend anymore.

A man who moves differently now.

Everything I'd learned—every bruise, every panic spiral, every D7 failure, every UTM welt, every breath Tim taught me to control, every night I carried fear home and still showed up again—all of it spoke through that one nod.

And something in me nodded back.

Because nothing happening is the best outcome.

And awareness—real, lived-in awareness—is the reason nothing happened.

You don't train to act.

You train so that when the world wobbles...you don't.

BACK HOME DEBRIEF

I didn't save anyone.

Didn't intervene.

Didn't step in.

I just didn't look away.

Most people live in Condition White.

It's not a flaw.

It's not weakness.

It's just the way modern life numbs us.

But comfort isn't safety.

And sleepwalking through your life is still sleepwalking.

You don't have to be a warrior.

You don't have to be tactical.

You don't have to be extraordinary.

Be intentional, go so far you can't go back, and fully commit to change in any form. The impact of every lesson echoed through my whole existence. This wasn't the plan; it was the outcome I didn't expect. However, I had to take these lessons from unconventional places so that you could absorb them and apply them truly. Thousands of perspectives exist on the subject, but doing was more impactful than the learning theory and trying to adjust my mentality or mindset; stress inoculation turned out to be my greatest teacher..

If I could talk to that nineteen-year-old kid on the curb—

the one holding a badge he didn't earn,

trying not to drown in his own heartbeat—

I wouldn't tell him to be brave.

I'd tell him to stay awake.

Because I see everything now.

— Erik

AUTHOR'S NOTE

I didn't write this book because I thought I had something to teach. I wrote it because for most of my life, I felt like I was one bad moment away from getting exposed.

Not as weak.

Not as incapable.

Just... untested.

Training didn't give me superpowers.

It didn't turn me into something I'm not.

It didn't erase fear, or doubt, or old tapes that still try to play when I'm tired.

What it gave me was clarity.

The kind you only earn when the world puts its thumb on the scale and asks who you really are when things tilt.

If you took anything from these pages, I hope it's this:

You don't have to chase danger.

You don't have to become tactical.

You don't have to put yourself through the grinder I did.

But you do have to wake up.

You do have to pay attention to the life you're walking through.

To the people you love.

To the moments you could have shown up — and the ones you almost didn't.

This book isn't a manual.

It's not a blueprint.

It's not a dare.

It's a reminder that you can start exactly where you are, with exactly what you have, and become someone your future self can nod back at without flinching.

I'm still learning.

Still screwing things up.

Still fighting the parts of myself that would rather hide, coast, or shut down.

But I'm awake now.

And if something in this story helped you lift your head a little higher, breathe a little deeper, or carry yourself through one moment you might have sleepwalked past before...then it was worth writing.

— Erik

ABOUT THE AUTHOR

Erik Weise is a father, a builder of capability, and a man who believes growth begins the moment comfort ends. In his early thirties, he stepped intentionally into a series of demanding tactical, mental, and physical training experiences—not to chase adrenaline, but to become the kind of man his sons could look to when life tilts.

A civilian with no military or law enforcement background, Erik chose to take himself into environments far outside his lane. The process reshaped him. Through pressure, fear, and disciplined self-work, he found clarity, resilience, and a new definition of what it means to be responsible for the people you love.

Today, he continues to train, learn, and push his own limits. His mission is simple: show his children that becoming better is a choice you make every day—and that stepping outside your comfort zone is where real transformation begins.

Bang to Boom is his first book.

DISCUSSION QUESTIONS — BANG TO BOOM

1.   What moment in the book made you realize you've been living in your own version of Condition White?

2.   Where have you been sleepwalking?

3.   Which chapter hit closest to home — and why do you think that moment landed the way it did? (Not what happened — what it revealed.)

4.   Where has comfort protected you...and where has it quietly cost you?

5.   What is the "hard thing" in your life you've been avoiding because it exposes an old fear?

6.   When was the last time you were tested and realized you weren't as ready as you thought?

7.   What did you do afterward?

8.   What part of Erik's transformation felt familiar, even if your path is different?

9.   If you were fully awake in your own life, what would change first? (Relationships? Health? Parenting? Work? Inner dialogue?)

10.   What was your personal 'D7' — the moment the mirror didn't lie?

11.   How does pressure shape you: do you collapse, overcompensate, or sharpen?

12.   What's one area of your life where you need to move from reaction to readiness?

13.   How do you want your children — or the younger version of you — to remember how you showed up under pressure?

14.   After reading this book, what is the first step you're willing to take outside your comfort zone?

RECOMMENDED READING AND FURTHER RESOURCES

These books and resources shaped the mindset behind Bang to Boom.

They are not tactical manuals — they are foundations for clarity, courage, and living wide awake.

Bang to Boom Field Notes (Substack)

There were moments from training that didn't make it into this book—stories that were too long, too raw, or still unfolding while I was writing. I keep those in a living field journal on Substack. It's the place where I break down the lessons behind the lessons, share what I'm training now, and talk through the things I'm still trying to figure out.

If any part of this book hit you in the chest, that's where the next chapter lives.

On Fear, Stress, and Performance

- "The Gift of Fear" by Gavin de Becker

- "On Combat" by Lt. Col. Dave Grossman

- "The Body Keeps the Score" by Bessel van der Kolk

- "Deep Survival" by Laurence Gonzales

On Awareness & Presence

- "Meditations" by Marcus Aurelius

- "The War of Art" by Steven Pressfield

- "The Obstacle Is the Way" by Ryan Holiday

On Masculinity, Responsibility & Behavior

- "Wild at Heart" by John Eldredge

- "Iron John" by Robert Bly

- "12 Rules for Life" by Jordan B. Peterson

On Growth, Grit, and Going Too Far

- "Can't Hurt Me" by David Goggins

- "Atomic Habits" by James Clear

- "Endure" by Alex Hutchinson

On Parenting & Legacy

- "Strong Fathers, Strong Daughters" by Meg Meeker

- "Raising Men" by Eric Davis

Every book on this list reflects the same idea at the heart of this story:

Growth is chosen, not stumbled into.

DISCLAIMER

(Please read before attempting anything regrettable.)

This memoir contains descriptions of real training events performed under professional supervision with real instructors whose job it is to keep people like me alive.

You?

You do not have a safety officer.

You have enthusiasm, an Amazon account, and a questionable group chat.

If, at any point during this book, you felt an urge to:

Kick open a door you forgot you don't own,

Practice "room clearing" in a Costco,

Simulate a hostage rescue using your Roomba,

Grapple your neighbor because he "looked like he needed pressure testing,"

Duct-tape a laser pointer to your dog and call it "movement drills,"

Fast-rope off your garage using a yoga strap,

Try a force-on-force scenario with your uncle who drinks Natural Light,

Or test your adrenal response by having your spouse attack you with a pool noodle while you're brushing your teeth,

...then I need you to understand something:

I am not responsible for you.

At all.

In any capacity.

Ever.

Every scenario in this book took place with:

Trained professionals

Controlled environments

Safety briefings

Medical staff

Actual rules

And zero people named "Chad" involved

If you attempt any of this without that infrastructure, you are no longer "embracing the warrior spirit."

You are auditioning for a viral video titled:

"Florida Man Attempts Urban Tactics, Immediately Regrets It."

Please do not:

Breach your pantry.

Stack up on your kids.

Run a Mogadishu Mile through your HOA.

Do vehicle extractions on sedans that aren't yours.

Recreate D7 with Nerf guns and blindfolds.

Or let your friend tase you "just so you can see what it feels like",

You are in charge of your own decisions.

Make good ones.

Or at least make ones that don't require explaining to EMTs.

This book is for entertainment, reflection, and maybe waking you up a little.

It is not a training manual.

It is not endorsed by any tactical instructors.

It is not responsible for your life choices, your injuries, or the footage your buddies upload without your consent.

Stay safe.

Stay smart.

Stay out of the news

CREDITS

Author

Erik Weise

A man powered by fear, breaching rams, and the gentle hum of panic attacks at inconvenient hours.

Any line in this book that made you gasp, laugh, or question my sanity:

Yeah. That happened.

I lived it.

You read it.

We're both tired now.

Story Development, Narrative Containment & Emergency Revisions

This book was built using the Bang → Boom → Breath method, which is the technical name for:

I did something catastrophically dumb, the universe yeeted a consequence at my face, and I tried breathing so I didn't disassociate into a houseplant.

All structural integrity was provided by Jarrod Weise, who dragged this story kicking and screaming into readability while whisper-yelling,

"BRO. HOW ARE YOU ALIVE?"

Ghostwriting, Emotional Damage Repair & Cinematic Chaos Control

Shaped using Mudhorn's Creative Intelligence Systems

Creative Strategy & Universe Engineering

Mudhorn Media LLC

 The crew responsible for turning

My trauma,

My training,

My desert hallucinations,

My breakthroughs,

My "oh no" moments,

And my brother's battle plans

Into a multi-phase cinematic universe nobody asked for and everyone will eventually fear.

Cover Design & Visual Identity

Inspired by the aesthetic:

"If a Nolan film elbow-dropped a self-help book while Sicario watched approvingly from the shadows."

Training Influences

Massive respect (and several outstanding apologies) to:

Marauders Tactical – Where humility goes to die and be reborn.

Sheepdog Response – Their special blend of terrifying people, the super friends of top tier instructors

Haley Strategic D7 – The room that knows what you fear and shows it to you in HD.

Force Options (Fred's kingdom) – Fred hopped into my truck like a cryptid and taught me to SEE, and I have not known peace since.

Technical Advisors

A shadowy cabal of professionals who kept this book factually correct, emotionally grounded, and free of phrases like "operator AF" or "tactically moist."

Every time I got something wrong, one of them materialized behind me like:

"Hey. Don't."

Beta Readers

Your feedback hurt.

Your enthusiasm is encouraging.

Your comments revealed things about me I was not prepared to confront.

Especially the one who wrote:

"I love it, but therapy is right there."

Noted.

Publishing & Production

Influence Foundry LLC

Mudhorn Media LLC

Printed through Kindle Direct Publishing, because apparently Bezos ships books faster than I can ship myself out of a bad situation.

Acknowledgment of Tools

This book was built with:

Sweat

Fear

Energy drinks

Regret

Mudhorn's IP (which probably violates several cosmic laws)

My two typing fingers

Divine intervention

And one entity who deserves an entire section

www.ingramcontent.com/pod-product-compliance
Lightning Source LLC
Chambersburg PA
CBHW010938120626
46554CB00008B/2512